CHRISTMAS
FROM THE HEART.

MEREDITH CORPORATION CONSUMER MARKETING
Director of Direct Marketing-Books: Daniel Fagan
Marketing Operations Manager: Max Daily
Assistant Marketing Manager: Kylie Dazzo

WATERBURY PUBLICATIONS, INC.
Contributing Editor: Carol Field Dahlstrom
Contributing Copy Editor: Peg Smith
Contributing Proofreader: Terri Fredrickson
Contributing Photographers: Jacob Fox, Jason Donnelly

Editorial Director: Lisa Kingsley
Creative Director: Ken Carlson
Associate Editor: Tricia Bergman
Associate Design Director: Doug Samuelson
Production Assistant: Mindy Samuelson

BETTER HOMES & GARDENS. MAGAZINE
Editor in Chief: Stephen Orr
Executive Editor: Oma Blaise Ford
Managing Editor: Gregory H. Kayko
Creative Director: Jennifer D. Madara
Food Editor: Jan Miller

MEREDITH CORPORATION
President and CEO: Tom Harty
Chairman: Stephen M. Lacy

Better Homes & Gardens®

CHRISTMAS
FROM THE HEART®

Volume 28

Meredith Consumer Marketing
Des Moines, Iowa

Contents

HOME FOR CHRISTMAS

There are songs about it, poems about it, and Christmas cards that use it as a theme. Yes, being home for Christmas is not just a place you go—it is a feeling in your heart as you transform your home into a holiday wonderland.

In this volume of *Christmas from the Heart,* we offer festive ideas, easy-does-it projects, and delicious kitchen goodies to make your home extra-special for the ones you love. You'll be amazed at the Christmas cookie recipes we have for you! Eggnog-Nut Thumbprint cookies and Creamy Cherry Dips look so inviting on your Christmas cookie tray, and Chocolate Waffle Turtle Cookies are perfect for your cookie exchange. Make plenty to share and enough to fill your kitchen cookie jar. For a cozy Christmas Eve night, stir up a pot of hearty Corn Chowder and serve it with warm No-Knead Skillet Focaccia.

If you like farmhouse-style, you'll love our Cozy Kitten Basket Liner (complete with kittens!) and our simple-to-stitch Hot-Chocolate Warmers. Want to keep things simple this year? We show you ways to make dazzling last-minute centerpieces and make-by-the-dozen greeting cards you're sure to love. Then return to Christmas past with sleek midcentury projects like a Throwback Tree Pillow and a Pom-Pom Stocking with all the charm of the 1950s. In our inspiring chapter "Home Sweet Holiday Home," you'll find an heirloom-quality Frosty Morning Gingerbread House you will want to appliqué and a Friendly Village Wreath to make with the kids. Fall in love with our sweet felt Woodland Friends and Beaded Wood Garland for your nature-inspired tree. We hope you are full of the Christmas spirit as you create a warm and holiday-filled place that everyone wants to come home to—a home that echoes the comfort and joy of a perfect *Christmas from the Heart.*

Merry Christmas!

Carol Field Dahlstrom

Warm and Cozy Farmhouse Christmas

Even if your home isn't tucked into a grove of trees or surrounded by outdoor friends in the barn, you can enjoy the charm of a cozy farmhouse Christmas wherever you celebrate.

HOT-CHOCOLATE WARMERS
Little pieces of farm-style gingham stitch up quickly into cloth coasters for warm-and-cozy hot chocolate.

WHAT YOU NEED FOR ONE COASTER
Two 8×8-inch squares of small-check, linenlike gingham
• 8×8-inch square of flannel • Thread to match fabrics
• Scissors • Needle • Red and green pearl cotton

WHAT YOU DO
1. Place gingham squares right sides together. Lay the flannel on top.
2. Using a ½-inch seam, stitch around the square, leaving a 2-inch opening for turning.
3. Trim seams and corners, then turn. Stitch opening closed. Press.
4. Thread the needle with red pearl cotton and using a running stitch, stitch around the edge of the coaster. Repeat using green pearl cotton. Knot and trim threads.

FARMHOUSE WELCOME

A vintage clothespin bag, once hung on an outside farmhouse clothesline, becomes the door decor for a holiday welcome. The bag is filled with small wrapped boxes and candy canes with a little tag clipped to the front. In place of a vintage bag, stitch a simple bag from worn denim jeans or a chambray shirt.

COZY KITTY BASKET LINER
Alphabet stamps spell out happy holiday combinations on a towel which then gets put to work as a simple basket liner for cute fluffy friends.

WHAT YOU NEED
Black-and-cream-stripe kitchen towel • Parchment paper • Masking tape • Pencil • Alphabet stamps and stamp pad

WHAT YOU DO
1. Lay the towel on a flat surface. Slide a small piece of parchment paper under the towel. Tape the towel to the surface to keep it smooth and tight.
2. To help with placement of the words, very lightly use a pencil to mark the beginning and end of the words that you plan to stamp. Choose combinations of holiday words like "hugs and kisses, cookies and milk, kitties and puppies, comfort and joy, Santa and Rudolph."
3. Press the alphabet stamps onto the stamp pad and press on the fabric. Let dry.

A MERRY CHRISTMAS FARMHOUSE TABLE
The traditional palette of red and green combines with farmhouse black-and-white stripes to create this simple-yet-stunning table setting to greet holiday family and friends.

SWEET & SIMPLE PLACE SETTING

A white dinner plate is the charger for vintage black-and-white enamelware plates. A streamer of red ribbon is tucked between the two plates. Napkins are wrapped with red-and-white bakers twine and a candy cane and mercury glass ornament are tied to the twine. A candy apple with crushed peppermint sprinkles completes the easy-to-create and very festive place setting.

CHALKBOARD GREETING

Welcome guests with a hand-drawn message that you can create in just a few minutes. Use black or charcoal chalkboard paint to paint a door in your home, or paint a smaller door to hang on the wall. Chalkboard paint is available at home stores in a variety of colors. Let the paint dry and then use a chalk marker pen to write a special Christmas message and decorative design on the door.

FRUIT & CANDLE CENTERPIECE:

*A shallow whitewashed basket is filled with Granny Smith apples and red pears.
Bits of greenery are tucked into the fruit. Place a candle in the middle of the basket on
a short glass holder before adding the fruit and greenery.*

BRODY'S CHRISTMAS DOG BED

Our best furry friend deserves a little Christmas comfort. Make a special doggy bed crafted from an old dresser drawer and give it a snazzy headboard using a garden fence section.

WHAT YOU NEED

Old dresser drawer • Wood filler • Sandpaper • Saw • White paint; paintbrush • Drapery rod ends • Drill and drill bit to fit size of bottom of fence piece • Small wire-style garden fence section (available at home and garden stores) • Glue • Pillowcase and small pillow or blankets • Ribbon

WHAT YOU DO

1. Choose a dresser drawer that fits your dog. Remove the pulls. Fill the holes with wood filler. Sand the surface until smooth.

2. Using the diagram as a guide, cut an opening on one side of the drawer. Sand the edges.

3. Paint the bed and let dry. Screw drapery rod ends into bottom of bed at corners for legs.

4. Drill small holes in the bottom or back of the drawer. Attach the wire fence headboard to the inside or outside of the drawer. Add glue to secure if needed.

5. Put the pillow or blankets inside pillowcase; put in the bed. Attach a ribbon around lower edge of the bed.

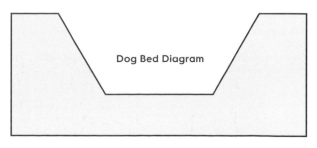

Dog Bed Diagram

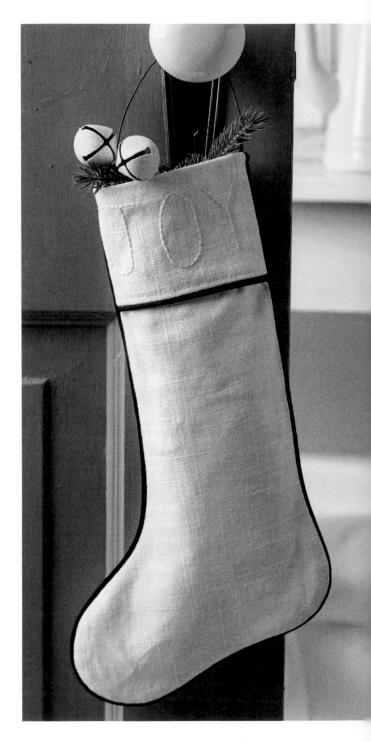

BLACK & WHITE INSPIRATION

Vintage or new black-and-white enamelware dishes are the inspiration for the stocking, above right, and other Christmas trims. Purchased striped towels and table runners set the tone for the holiday displays.

ENAMELWARE-INSPIRED STOCKING

Love the contrast of black-and-white enamelware? Take it a step further by stitching a look-alike stocking to enjoy at Christmastime. The stocking is stitched from white linenlike fabric, then finished with black piping trim. White on white embroidery stitched on the cuff spells out a greeting or name.

WHAT YOU NEED FOR ONE STOCKING

½ yard white linenlike fabric • Transfer paper • Black piping • Thread to match fabrics • White embroidery floss • Needle • Scissors • Fine black wire

WHAT YOU DO

1. Enlarge and copy the stocking and cuff templates, below and right. Cut out on solid line.

2. Fold fabric in half, right sides together, and trace stocking and cuff on fabric. Cut out.

3. Transfer the letters on front cuff piece using transfer paper. Using white embroidery floss, stitch the letters using the Stem Stitch. (See page 160). Turn under bottom edge of cuff and stitch the piping to the bottom edge.

4. Lay piped cuff on top of the stocking front, aligning raw edges and treating the piece as one. Pin piping, raw edge to raw edge, to align with ½-inch seamline on stocking. Baste in place. With right sides facing, stitch stocking together, catching the piping in the seam, leaving the top open for turning. Turn and press.

5. Turn under the top of the stocking and stitch raw edge down.

6. Make loops at the end of the wire and whip-stitch in place at each side.

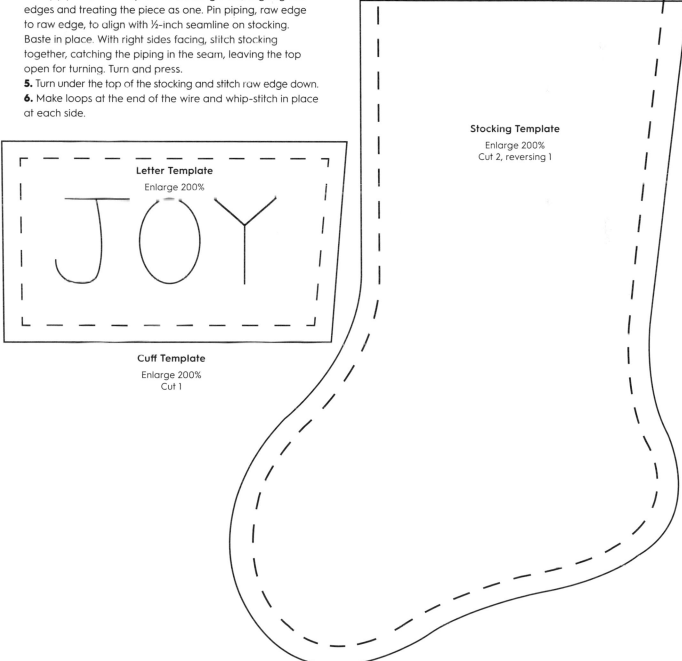

Enamelware-Inspired
Stocking Templates

Stocking Template
Enlarge 200%
Cut 2, reversing 1

Letter Template
Enlarge 200%

JOY

Cuff Template
Enlarge 200%
Cut 1

FRAMED-PAPER TRAY

*A vintage tray is painted black and a piece of Christmas wrapping paper is framed
in the tray. Choose a paper that coordinates with the black frame and back the paper
with cardboard. Place a candle in a coffee pot or other piece of enamelware and set on
the tray to complete the look.*

RUBBER BAND TRIMS

Humble rubber bands help create a design technique for simple-to-make holiday ornaments.

WHAT YOU NEED

Soft green matte-finish one-color ornaments • Clear spray paint • Wide rubber bands • White spray paint • Pencil • Jars or glasses

WHAT YOU DO

1. Carefully spray the ornaments with clear spray paint. Let dry.

2. Wrap the rubber bands around the ornament to crisscross. Spray with white spray paint. Thread a pencil through the ornament hanger and rest them between two jars or glasses to dry.

3. Carefully remove the rubber bands.

WHITEWASHED KITTY BASKET

A woven basket is whitewashed and embellished with jingle bells for a charming wrap to present a new pet. Simply brush on a touch of white acrylic paint and then tie on a trio of jingle bells. Line the basket with a flannel square of fabric. Then present the little kitten to his new friend.

SOFT-TOUCH COUNTRY WREATH

Torn pieces of small-print fabric are tucked together on a hoop wreath frame for a country-style holiday wreath.

WHAT YOU NEED

Four ⅛-yard pieces of small print cotton fabric in neutral colors • Wire wreath form with three tiers (see Sources, page 160) • Scissors • 12-inch length of narrow leather cording

WHAT YOU DO

1. Tear the fabric into strips about ½ to ¾ inches wide and 4 inches long. Strips can vary in width and length.
2. Plan the design and placement of the fabric and tie to the wreath form.
3. When complete, trim the strips to be similar in length if desired.
4. Loop cording around the back of the form for hanging.

PROPELLER WREATH

For a clever country spin on the wreath, bring an old propeller into play. Rusted to a burnished complexion, this 18-inch propeller comes to life when clumps of tiny Cremnosedum 'Little Gem' are glued to the center. The leaves will last a few weeks without shriveling, but they don't like cold so it's best to hang the wreath indoors.

RUSTIC SPLATTER ORNAMENTS

Basic red ornaments become miniature works of art when they are splattered with paint. Display them in vintage bed springs for a rustic country look.

WHAT YOU NEED

Large red ornaments • Spray paint in gray, gold, and black • Small sponge • White, gold, and black craft paint • Paper plate • Toothbrush • Small paintbrush • Bakers twine

WHAT YOU DO

1. Be sure the ornaments are clean and dry.
2. Spray ornaments with gray paint. Rub some off with a sponge. Repeat using the gold paint until desired look is achieved. Let dry.
3. Put crafts paint on a paper plate then dip the toothbrush into the paint. Spatter it on the ornament. Let dry.
4. Spray paint the hanger of the ornament black. Let dry.
5. Thread twine through the hanger.

RUSTIC FUNNEL TREE

Search Grandpa's workshop to find vintage funnels to stack and make into a clever little Christmas tree.

WHAT YOU NEED

Vintage metal funnels in 3 sizes • Hot glue and hot-glue gun • Cotton lace • Cream and gray ribbon

WHAT YOU DO

1. Plan the design by experimenting with stacking the funnels.
2. Run a line of hot glue around the inside of the mouth of the funnels. Place the lace on the glue to secure.
3. Stack the funnels, tie a bow, and glue at the top.

DRESSED UP CORNER

Rail storage takes on vintage holiday magic with a few cypress sprigs and miniature garlands of mercury glass pinecones and cotton balls threaded on fishing line. A white knitted stocking replaces the dish towel usually hanging in this spot.

Cookie Exchange

Fill cookie platters and spread holiday cheer to friends, family, and co-workers with a few sweet selections from this collection of festive treats.

APRICOT-ALMOND KOLACHES

Cardamom-spiced apricot jam is the filling for these traditional Czechoslovakian treats. Cream cheese in the dough makes the pastry extra-tender.

WHAT YOU NEED
- 1 cup butter, softened
- 1 8-oz. pkg. cream cheese, softened
- 2 cups all-purpose flour
- ⅔ cup apricot jam
- ¼ tsp. ground cardamom
- 2 Tbsp. sliced almonds
- 1 cup powdered sugar
- 4 tsp. milk
- ¼ tsp. almond extract

WHAT YOU DO
1. In a large bowl beat butter and cream cheese with a mixer on medium until light and fluffy. Gradually beat in flour. Divide dough into two portions; cover and chill 2 hours or until easy to handle.

2. Preheat oven to 400°F. In a small bowl stir together the jam and cardamom. On a lightly floured surface roll one portion of dough into a 15×9-inch rectangle. Cut into 3-inch squares. Place 1 tsp. of the jam mixture in center of each square. Sprinkle with a few almonds. Overlap two opposite corners of dough to meet in the center; pinch tightly to seal. (Or overlap all four corners of dough over filling and pinch tightly to seal. Or cut 3-inch rounds and top with jam and almonds.) Place 2 inches apart on ungreased cookie sheets. Repeat with remaining dough and jam mixture.

3. Bake 10 to 12 minutes or until bottoms are lightly browned. Cool on cookie sheet 1 minute. Remove; cool on wire racks.

4. For icing, in a small bowl stir together powdered sugar, milk, and almond extract. Drizzle icing over kolaches. Makes 30 cookies.

CHOCOLATE-GLAZED MADELEINES

These shell-shape cookies have the delicate texture of a sponge cake. They require a special pan, but the number of variations on this French cookie makes the purchase worth it if you do a lot of baking.

WHAT YOU NEED
- ½ cup all-purpose flour
- ½ tsp. baking powder
- ⅛ tsp. baking soda
- ⅛ tsp. salt
- ½ cup sugar
- 2 egg yolks
- ½ cup butter, melted and cooled
- ½ tsp. orange zest
- 1 Tbsp. orange liqueur or orange juice
- 1 tsp. vanilla
- 2 egg whites, lightly beaten
- 1 recipe Chocolate Glaze
  Finely chopped pistachio nuts (optional)

WHAT YOU DO
1. Preheat oven to 375°F. Grease and flour twenty-four 3-inch madeleine molds. In a small bowl stir together first four ingredients (through salt).

2. In a medium bowl beat sugar and egg yolks with a mixer on medium until combined. Beat in next four ingredients (through vanilla) on low until smooth. Sprinkle flour mixture, about one-fourth at a time, over yolk mixture; stir in gently. Gently stir in egg whites. Spoon batter into prepared molds, filling each about half full.

3. Bake 10 to 12 minutes or until edges are golden and tops spring back when lightly touched. Cool in molds 1 minute. Using a knife tip, loosen cookies from molds. Invert molds onto wire racks. Remove molds, cool cookies.

4. Dip half of each cookie in warm Chocolate Glaze. If desired, sprinkle with pistachios. Chill 30 minutes or until set. Makes 24 cookies.

Chocolate Glaze In a small heavy saucepan bring ½ cup heavy cream, 1 Tbsp. orange liqueur (if desired), and ½ tsp. vanilla just to boiling over medium-high heat. Remove from heat. Add 6 oz. chopped bittersweet or semisweet chocolate (do not stir). Let stand 5 minutes. Stir until smooth.

EGGNOG-NUT THUMBPRINTS

These festive cookies are filled with a rum-flavor buttercream. To create a pretty presentation, use a pastry bag fitted with a star tip to pipe it into the centers of the cookies.

WHAT YOU NEED

- ¾ cup butter, softened
- ½ cup sugar
- ⅛ tsp. ground nutmeg
- 2 egg yolks
- 1 tsp. vanilla
- 1½ cups all-purpose flour
- 2 egg whites, lightly beaten
- 1½ cups finely chopped walnuts
- 1 recipe Rum Filling
  Grated whole nutmeg or ground nutmeg (optional)

WHAT YOU DO

1. In a large bowl beat butter with a mixer on medium 30 seconds. Add sugar and ⅛ tsp. nutmeg. Beat until combined, scraping bowl as needed. Beat in egg yolks and vanilla. Beat in flour. If necessary, cover and chill dough until easy to handle (about 1 hour).

2. Preheat oven to 375°F. Grease a cookie sheet. Shape dough into 1-inch balls. Roll balls in egg whites, then in walnuts; place 1 inch apart on prepared cookie sheet. Press thumb in center of each ball.

3. Bake 12 to 15 minutes or until edges are light brown. If centers puff during baking, re-press with a spoon. Transfer cookies to cool on a wire rack.

4. Pipe or spoon about ½ tsp. Rum Filling into center of each cookie. If desired, sprinkle with grated nutmeg. Makes 40 cookies.

Rum Filling In a medium bowl beat ¼ cup softened butter with a mixer on medium 30 seconds. Add 1 cup powdered sugar and 1 tsp. rum or ¼ tsp. rum extract. Beat until fluffy, scraping bowl as needed. Beat in 1 to 2 tsp. milk to reach spreading consistency.

PEPPERMINT-SPRINKLE PALMIERS

The confetti-inspired decoration of these cream cheese-filled spiraled butter cookies makes them pop visually on a packed cookie platter. (Pictured on page 29.)

WHAT YOU NEED

½   cup butter, softened
½   cup granulated sugar
½   cup packed brown sugar
½   tsp. baking powder
¼   tsp. salt
1   egg
3   Tbsp. milk
½   tsp. vanilla
2½   cups all-purpose flour
1   8-oz. pkg. cream cheese, softened
½   cup powdered sugar
     Few drops red food coloring
¼   cup crushed peppermint candies
½   cup red sprinkles (jimmies)
8   oz. white baking chocolate, chopped
2   tsp. shortening

WHAT YOU DO

1. In a large bowl beat butter with a mixer on medium 30 seconds. Add granulated and brown sugars, baking powder, and salt. Beat until combined, scraping bowl as needed. Beat in egg, 2 Tbsp. milk, and the vanilla. Beat in 2¼ cups flour. Divide dough in half.

2. For filling, in a medium bowl beat cream cheese, powdered sugar, remaining ¼ cup flour, and remaining 1 Tbsp. milk on low to medium until smooth. Tint pale pink with food coloring.

3. On a lightly floured surface, roll one portion of dough into a 12×8-inch rectangle. Spread with half the filling to within ½ inch of edges. Sprinkle with 2 Tbsp. peppermint candies and top with 2 Tbsp. sprinkles. Roll both long edges toward center, scroll fashion, to meet in center. Brush seam where dough meets with additional milk; press to seal. Repeat with remaining dough, filling, peppermint candies and sprinkles. Wrap each roll in plastic wrap. Freeze 1 to 2 hours or until firm enough to slice.

4. Preheat oven to 350°F. Grease a cookie sheet or line with parchment paper. Using a serrated knife, cut rolls into ¼-inch slices. Place 1 inch apart on prepared cookie sheet. Bake 10 minutes or until edges are light brown. Remove; cool on a wire rack.

5. In a small bowl microwave white chocolate and shortening 1 minute or until melted and smooth, stirring twice. Dip a portion of each cookie into melted white chocolate, allowing excess to drip off. Place dipped cookies on waxed paper. Top with remaining ¼ cup sprinkles; let stand until chocolate is set. Makes 68 cookies.

ESPRESSO BALLS

The flavors of chocolate, coffee, and hazelnut come together in these rich treats studded with a chocolate-covered coffee bean.

WHAT YOU NEED

1   cup butter, softened
½   cup powdered sugar
¼   cup unsweetened cocoa powder
1   Tbsp. coffee liqueur
1   tsp. vanilla
1¾   cups all-purpose flour
1½   cups hazelnuts (filberts), toasted and ground*
¼   cup chocolate-covered coffee beans, ground
     Whole chocolate-covered coffee beans, for garnish

WHAT YOU DO

1. Preheat oven to 325°F. In a large bowl beat butter with a mixer on medium to high 30 seconds. Add powdered sugar and cocoa powder; beat until combined. Beat in coffee liqueur and vanilla. Beat in as much flour as you can with the mixer. Stir in any remaining flour, ½ cup of the ground hazelnuts, and the ground coffee beans.

2. Shape dough into 1-inch balls. Roll in remaining ground nuts. Place balls 2 inches apart on ungreased cookie sheets.

3. Bake 15 minutes or until bottoms are light brown. Lightly press a whole chocolate-covered coffee bean into the top of each cookie. Cool on cookie sheets on wire racks 3 minutes. Transfer to wire racks; let cool. Makes 54 cookies.

*Tip To toast hazelnuts, preheat oven to 350°F. Spread nuts in a shallow baking pan. Bake 8 to 10 minutes or until lightly toasted. Cool slightly; place on a clean kitchen towel. Rub nuts with towel to remove loose skins. Pulse cooled nuts in a food processor until the consistency of cornmeal.

*Tip If you prefer, use the microwave to melt the candy coating. In a small microwave-safe bowl combine candy coating and shortening. Microwave on high 30 to 60 seconds or until coating is melted and mixture is smooth, stirring every 30 seconds.

To Store Layer dipped and sprinkled sandwich cookies between sheets of waxed paper in an airtight container; cover. Store in the refrigerator up to 2 days. Do not freeze.

MINTY COCOA-FUDGE SANDWICH COOKIES

Dutch-process cocoa is slightly mellower and lighter in color than regular cocoa powder, so choose which you use according to your taste. Regular cocoa powder produces a more intense chocolate flavor than Dutch-process.

WHAT YOU NEED

3½ cups all-purpose flour
⅔ cup unsweetened Dutch-process or regular cocoa powder
2 tsp. baking powder
1⅓ cups butter, softened
1½ cups sugar
¼ cup vegetable oil
2 eggs
1 Tbsp. vanilla
1 14-oz. can sweetened condensed milk
1 10-oz. pkg. mint-flavor semisweet chocolate chips*
2 oz. unsweetened chocolate, coarsely chopped

WHAT YOU DO

1. In a medium bowl stir together flour, cocoa powder, and baking powder. In a large bowl beat butter with a mixer on medium 30 seconds. Add sugar and oil. Beat until combined, scraping bowl as needed. Beat in eggs and vanilla until combined. Beat in flour mixture. Cover and chill 1 hour or until dough is easy to handle.

2. Preheat oven to 350°F. Shape dough into 1-inch balls. Place 2 inches apart on an ungreased cookie sheet. Dip bottom of a glass in additional sugar and slightly flatten each ball. Bake 7 to 9 minutes or just until firm. Remove; cool on a wire rack.

3. For filling, in a small saucepan combine sweetened condensed milk, chocolate chips, and chopped chocolate. Stir over medium heat until chocolate is melted; cool.

4. Spread about 1 tsp. filling on bottoms of half of the cookies. Top with remaining cookies, bottom sides down. Makes 36 cookies.

*Tip In place of mint-flavor semisweet chocolate chips, use 1½ cups regular semisweet chocolate chips and stir ¼ tsp. mint extract into the melted chocolate.

CREAMY CHERRY DIPS

Vanilla wafers are sandwiched together with a cherry-cream cheese filling and dipped in chocolate to create these simple no-bake treats.

WHAT YOU NEED

½ 8-oz. pkg. cream cheese, softened
½ cup powdered sugar
½ cup finely chopped, drained maraschino cherries
¼ tsp. almond extract
60 vanilla wafers
12 oz. chocolate-flavor candy coating, coarsely chopped
2 tsp. shortening
Jimmies or decors

WHAT YOU DO

1. For filling, in a medium bowl beat cream cheese and powdered sugar with a mixer on medium until smooth. Stir in cherries and almond extract. Spread filling on bottoms of 30 vanilla wafers. Top with remaining wafers, bottom sides down. Cover and chill 30 minutes or until filling is firm.

2. In a medium saucepan stir chocolate candy coating and shortening over low heat until melted and smooth. Remove from heat. Using a fork, dip each sandwich cookie in melted chocolate coating, turning to coat completely and letting excess coating drip back into pan. Place dipped cookies on waxed paper. Sprinkle with jimmies. Let stand 30 minutes or until chocolate coating is set. Makes 30 cookies.

CRYSTALLIZED GINGER-AND-ORANGE ICEBOX COOKIES

The beauty of icebox cookies is that the dough can be made ahead and you can simply slice and bake when you need them—and as many as you need at a time.

WHAT YOU NEED
½   cup butter, softened
¾   cup granulated sugar
1½ tsp. baking powder
⅛   tsp. salt
1   egg
2   cups all-purpose flour
⅓   cup finely chopped crystallized ginger
4   tsp. orange zest
¾   cup coarse white decorating sugar

WHAT YOU DO
1. In a large bowl beat butter with a mixer on medium to high 30 seconds. Add granulated sugar, baking powder, and salt. Beat on medium until combined. Beat in egg. Beat in as much flour as you can. Stir in any remaining flour, the crystallized ginger, and orange zest.
2. Divide dough into three portions. Shape each portion into a 7-inch log. Coat logs in decorating sugar. Wrap each in plastic wrap or waxed paper. Chill dough until firm enough to slice (about 4 hours).
3. Preheat oven to 350°F. Lightly grease a cookie sheet. With a serrated knife, cut logs into ¼-inch slices; place 1 inch apart on prepared cookie sheet. Sprinkle with some remaining decorating sugar.
4. Bake 8 to 10 minutes or until bottoms are light brown. Transfer to wire racks to cool completely. Makes 70 cookies.

CHOCOLATE WAFFLE TURTLE COOKIES

These whimsical waffle cookies feature all the flavors of classic turtle candies—chocolate, caramel, and pecans.

WHAT YOU NEED
1   cup butter or margarine, melted
1½   cups granulated sugar
4   eggs, lightly beaten
½   cup unsweetened cocoa powder
2   tsp. vanilla
2   cups all-purpose flour
¼   cup butter
3   Tbsp. water
3   Tbsp. unsweetened cocoa powder
1½   cups powdered sugar
1   tsp. vanilla
½   cup caramel ice cream topping
1   cup chopped toasted pecans (optional)

WHAT YOU DO
1. Preheat waffle iron to medium-high (if temperature settings are available). In a large bowl stir together melted butter, granulated sugar, eggs, ½ cup cocoa powder, and 2 tsp. vanilla. Add flour; stir just until combined.
2. Drop heaping teaspoonfuls of batter into center of each waffle grid. Bake 2 minutes, adjusting heat as necessary. Using a fork, transfer cookies to wire racks to cool completely. Repeat with remaining batter.
3. For the glaze, in a small saucepan heat ¼ cup butter and the water over low heat until butter is melted. Stir in 3 Tbsp. cocoa powder until smooth. Remove from heat. Beat in powdered sugar and 1 tsp. vanilla. Stir in additional hot water, if needed, to reach drizzling consistency. Drizzle glaze and caramel topping over cookies. Sprinkle with pecans, if desired. Makes 48 cookies.

GINGERBREAD STARS

A sprinkle of shimmery silver and gold coarse decorating sugars makes these gingery cookies twinkle.

WHAT YOU NEED

3	cups all-purpose flour
2	tsp. ground ginger
1	tsp. baking soda
½	tsp. salt
½	tsp. ground cinnamon
½	tsp. ground cloves
½	cup butter, softened
¼	cup shortening
¾	cup sugar
½	cup molasses
1	egg
1	recipe Powdered Sugar Icing
	Silver and gold coarse sugars

WHAT YOU DO

1. In a medium bowl stir together flour, ginger, baking soda, salt, cinnamon, and cloves. Set aside.

2. In a bowl beat butter and shortening with a mixer on medium to high 30 seconds. Add sugar and molasses; beat until combined. Add egg; beat well. Add flour mixture; beat on low just until combined. Divide dough in half; cover and chill 3 hours or until easy to handle.

3. Preheat oven to 375°F. Lightly grease cookie sheets. On a well-floured surface, roll half the dough at a time to ⅛-inch thickness. Using a 3- to 4-inch star-shape cookie cutter, cut into shapes. Place 1 inch apart on prepared cookie sheets.

4. Bake 5 to 7 minutes or until edges are very light brown. Cool on cookie sheet 1 minute. Transfer cookies to a wire rack to cool completely.

5. Spread Powdered Sugar Icing on each cookie and decorate with silver and gold sugars. Let stand 1 hour or until icing is set. Makes 26 to 30 cookies.

Powdered Sugar Icing In a bowl stir together 1½ cups powdered sugar, ¼ tsp. vanilla extract, and 2 Tbsp. milk.

CHOCOLATY MELTING SNOWMEN

These cute cookies will bring smiles to the faces of friends and family. A puddle of vanilla-flavor candy coating and a few candies create the illusion of a sweet snowman melting away.

WHAT YOU NEED

½   cup shortening
½   cup peanut butter
½   cup granulated sugar
½   cup packed brown sugar
¼   cup unsweetened cocoa powder
1   tsp. baking powder
¼   tsp. salt
⅛   tsp. baking soda
1   egg
3   Tbsp. milk
½   tsp. vanilla
1½ cups all-purpose flour
16 oz. vanilla-flavor candy coating, coarsely chopped
20 bite-size chocolate-covered peanut butter cups
    Miniature chocolate chips and orange sprinkles

WHAT YOU DO

1. Preheat oven to 350°F. In a large bowl beat shortening and peanut butter with a mixer on medium 30 seconds. Add sugars, cocoa powder, baking powder, salt, and baking soda. Beat until combined, scraping bowl as needed. Beat in egg, milk, and vanilla. Beat in flour.

2. Shape dough into 20 balls; place 2 inches apart on an ungreased cookie sheet.

3. Bake 9 to 11 minutes or just until edges are firm. Cool on cookie sheet 2 minutes. Transfer cookies to a wire rack to cool completely.

4. In a medium-size microwave-safe bowl heat candy coating on medium 2½ to 3 minutes, stirring every 30 seconds, until melted and smooth.

5. For snowmen, spoon melted coating onto cookies to resemble melting snow. While coating is tacky, add peanut butter cups for top hats, mini chocolate chips for eyes, and orange sprinkles for noses. Makes 20 cookies.

RED PLUM SHORTBREAD BARS

Shaping the buttery dough into rectangles that can be sliced makes quick work of shortbread. A splash of port wine deepens the flavor and adds a festive touch to the plum jam filling.

WHAT YOU NEED

1   cup butter, softened
⅔   cup granulated sugar
2¼   cups all-purpose flour
⅔   cup red plum jam
2   Tbsp. Port wine (optional)
1   cup powdered sugar
2   Tbsp. milk
1   tsp. vanilla

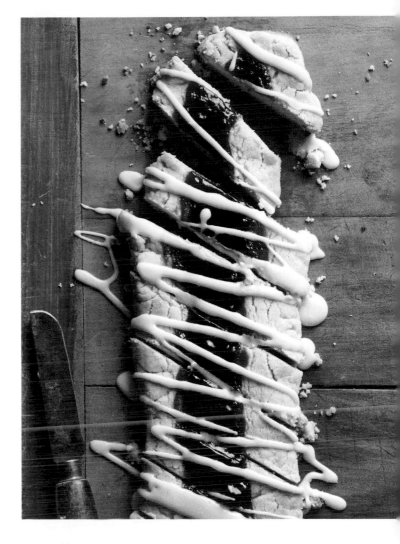

WHAT YOU DO

1. Preheat oven to 350°F. In a large bowl beat butter with a mixer on medium 30 seconds. Add granulated sugar. Beat until combined, scraping bowl as needed. Gradually beat in flour on low just until combined. Knead until dough comes together (dough will be crumbly).

2. Divide dough in half. On a large ungreased baking pan shape each half into a 12×2-inch rectangle, allowing 4 inches between rolls. Press ¼-inch deep indentations down the center of each rectangle. In a small bowl stir together the jam and Port wine (if using). Spoon half the jam mixture into indentations; set aside remaining jam mixture.

3. Bake 15 minutes. Remove from oven; spoon on remaining jam mixture. Bake 5 minutes more or until edges are lightly browned. Cool slightly on baking pan on a wire rack. Transfer to a cutting board; cut into 1-inch diagonal strips (do not separate strips). Cool completely.

4. In a small bowl stir together powdered sugar, milk, and vanilla. Add more milk as needed to reach drizzling consistency. Drizzle over bars. Makes 26 bars.

PEPPERMINT CREAM BARS

These no-bake bars bring together two favorite flavors—peppermint and chocolate—that play very well together.

WHAT YOU NEED

1   14.3-oz. pkg. chocolate sandwich cookies with white filling (36 cookies)
⅓   cup butter, melted
4   cups powdered sugar
¼   cup butter, softened
¼   cup milk
½   tsp. peppermint extract
12   oz. semisweet chocolate, coarsely chopped
1   Tbsp. shortening

WHAT YOU DO

1. Preheat oven to 350°F. Line a 13×9-inch baking pan with foil, extending foil over edges. For crust, place cookies in a food processor. Cover and process until very finely chopped. In a medium bowl combine chopped cookies and ⅓ cup melted butter. Press mixture into prepared pan. Bake 12 minutes or until set. Cool in pan on a wire rack.

2. Meanwhile, for peppermint filling, in a large bowl beat powdered sugar and ¼ cup softened butter with a mixer on low until butter is evenly distributed. Add milk and peppermint extract; beat until smooth. Spread filling over crust. Freeze 45 minutes.

3. In a medium-size microwave-safe bowl combine chocolate and shortening. Microwave 1 to 2 minutes or until chocolate is melted and smooth, stirring every 30 seconds. Cool 15 minutes. Spread melted chocolate over peppermint filling. Chill 15 minutes or until chocolate is firm. Using edges of foil, lift out uncut bars. Cut into bars. Makes 36 bars.

COCONUT-SUGAR COOKIE BARS WITH COCONUT-LIME FROSTING

If you are garnishing with flaked coconut and would like it toasted to enhance the flavor, spread the flakes in a single layer on a rimmed baking sheet and toast in a 350°F oven 5 to 10 minutes until golden, stirring once, and watching carefully to avoid burning.

WHAT YOU NEED

    Nonstick cooking spray
3   cups all-purpose flour
1   Tbsp. cornstarch
1   tsp. baking powder
½   tsp. salt
¼   tsp. baking soda
1   cup butter, softened
1¼   cups sugar
1   egg
2   Tbsp. sour cream
1   tsp. vanilla
½   tsp. coconut extract
1   recipe Coconut-Lime Frosting
    Flaked coconut and/or lime zest (optional)

WHAT YOU DO

1. Preheat oven to 350°F. Line a 13×9-inch baking pan with foil, extending foil over edges of pan. Coat foil with cooking spray. In a medium bowl stir together flour, cornstarch, baking powder, salt, and baking soda; set aside.

2. In a large bowl beat butter with a mixer on medium to high 30 seconds. Add sugar; beat until combined, scraping bowl as needed. Beat in egg, sour cream, vanilla, and coconut extract. Gradually beat in flour. Transfer dough to prepared pan. Press dough evenly into pan.

3. Bake 20 to 25 minutes or until light golden brown on edges. Cool in pan on a wire rack. Use foil to lift uncut bars out of pan. Spread with Coconut-Lime Frosting. If desired, sprinkle with flaked coconut and lime zest. Cut into bars. Makes 48 bars.

Coconut-Lime Frosting In a large bowl beat 1 cup butter, softened, with a mixer on medium to high 30 seconds. Gradually beat in 3½ cups powdered sugar until smooth. Beat in 1 tsp. lime zest, 1 tsp. lime juice, and ¼ tsp. coconut extract.

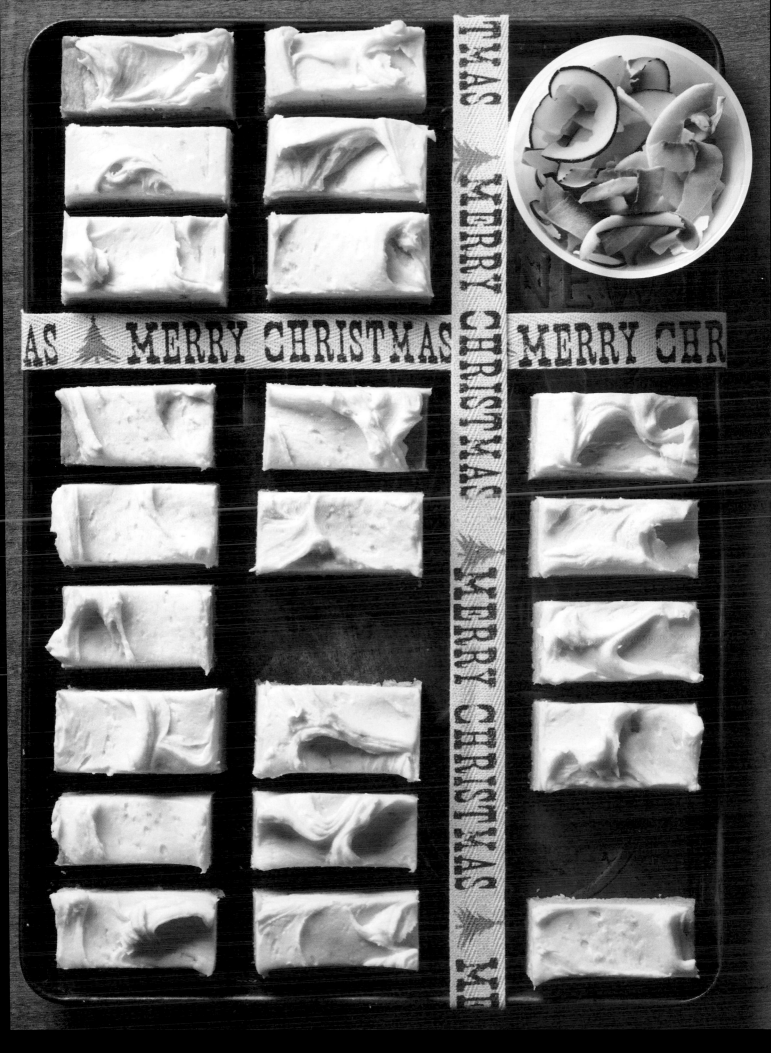

Midcentury Merry

The modernism of the 1950s and '60s creates a backdrop for clean, midcentury Christmas designs with timeless color and flair. Celebrate this Christmas-past look in your modern holiday home with look-alike designs from that happy time.

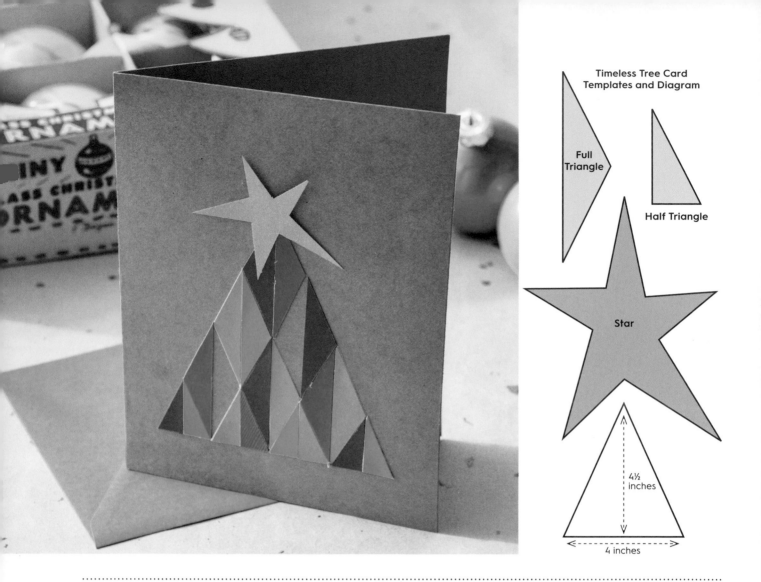

**Timeless Tree Card
Templates and Diagram**

Full Triangle

Half Triangle

Star

4½ inches

4 inches

TIMELESS TREE CARD

Simple shapes stack up to make a classic Christmas tree motif using a variety of holiday colors.

WHAT YOU NEED

Blank neutral color card and envelope in desired color (our card is 5½×7½ inches) • Pencil • Cardstock in various shades of green and brown • Gold cardstock • Scissors • Spray adhesive

WHAT YOU DO

1. Lay the card on a flat surface and mark where the tree will be placed at top and bottom. The tree will be about 4½ inches high.
2. Using the templates, above right, and various colors of cardstock, cut 10 of each (full triangle) and 8 of each (half triangle) pieces.
3. Arrange the pieces on the card, adjusting as desired.
4. Using spray adhesive, adhere the triangles onto the front of the card. Using the star template, cut a star from gold cardstock and glue to the top of the tree.

SLEEK TREE CANDLES

Uncluttered lines and simple shapes from midcentury design are the inspiration for these colorful Christmas candles.

WHAT YOU NEED

Tree candle mold (See Sources, page 160) • Coconut oil or mold release • Soy wax • Liquid candle coloring drops • Candle wicking

WHAT YOU DO

1. Prep the mold by spraying with mold release or coating with coconut oil then secure candle wick in place.
2. Melt the wax in a double boiler, stirring frequently. Watch carefully so the wax does not overheat. **Note**: Wax can explode if heated to high temperatures.
3. When wax is melted, separate the wax into separate containers and add drops of coloring until wax is desired color.
4. Pour the wax into the mold and let it cool completely.
5. Release the candles from the molds.

Never leave a burning candle unattended.

LAYERED FELT ORNAMENTS

Layers of midcentury colors create one-of-a-kind ornaments that let the Christmas light shine through.

WHAT YOU NEED

Nonwoven felt, such as National Nonwovens in assorted colors • Scissors • Spray adhesive • Ribbon • Fine gold thread for hanging

WHAT YOU DO

1. Referring to the templates, below, cut one of each template (ornament base, ornament top, and ornament bottom) and three of diamonds for each ornament, using different colors of felt.

2. Attach the ornament top, ornament bottom, and diamonds on top of ornament base using spray adhesive, placing the thread for hanging between the ornament top layer and ornament base layer.

3. Press if desired.

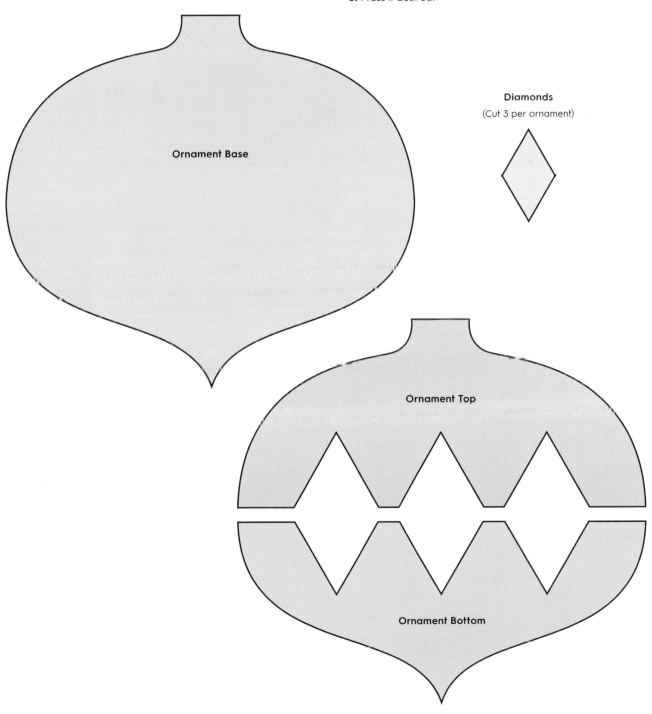

Ornament Base

Diamonds

(Cut 3 per ornament)

Ornament Top

Ornament Bottom

THROWBACK TREE PILLOW

Crisp lines, a midcentury palette, and Sputnik-like angles make this pillow a holiday decorating treasure.

WHAT YOU NEED

Nonwoven felt, such as National Nonwovens in teal, seafoam green, pink and assorted colors • One small pom-pom • 14 inches or desired size pillow form • Iron-on fusible webbing • Hot-glue gun and glue sticks • Sewing machine • Scissors

WHAT YOU DO

1. Measure pillow form. Cut two pieces from teal felt, 2 inches larger than pillow form measurements. Cut one piece from seafoam felt, half the width and the full height of the previous measurement. Using iron-on fusible web, attach the seafoam felt to the teal felt.

2. Enlarge and copy template below. To create the tree, cut pieces from various colors and arrange on the pillow as shown in the diagram. Use iron-on fusible web to attach pieces to pillow form.

3. Using a hot-glue gun and glue, attach pom-pom to the top of the tree.

4. With right sides together, sew around the perimeter of the pillow cover leaving a 6-inch opening on the bottom. Turn right side out. Place pillow form in opening and hand sew pillow closed.

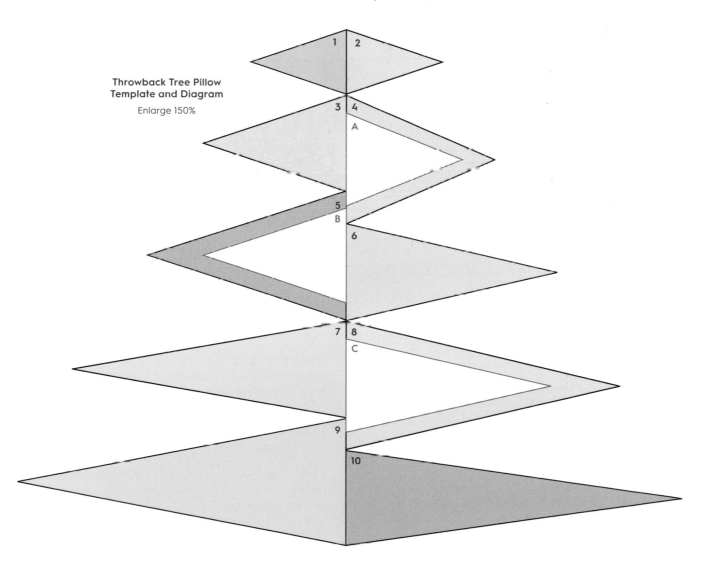

Throwback Tree Pillow Template and Diagram

Enlarge 150%

COPYCAT PACKAGES

The fabrics from the 1950s and 1960s were graphic and oftentimes colorful. Copy these beautiful fabrics onto paper and use them to wrap your Christmas gifts for an easy and fun retro look.

WHAT YOU NEED

Midcentury fabrics with small prints, such as tablecloths, aprons, and tea towels • Copy machine • White paper • Ribbons, bakers twine, jingle bells • Scissors

WHAT YOU DO

1. Choose colorful holiday midcentury fabrics that have small prints.
2. Place the fabric on a color copy machine and use the color setting to copy the fabric onto the paper. **Note:** The fabric should be copyright free if it is more than 50 years.
3. Wrap the package with the paper and embellish with ribbon, twine, and jingle bells.

POM-POM STOCKING

Vintage fabric stitches up easily into a colorful stocking with pom-pom trim that poses nicely alongside a vintage aluminum tree.

WHAT YOU NEED

Pencil • Tracing paper • Scissors • ¼ yard midcentury print fabric • White ball fringe • Thread to match fabrics

WHAT YOU DO

1. Enlarge and trace the templates, opposite, and cut out. Cut two stocking patterns from print fabric, reversing one.
2. For the cuff, cut one piece.
3. With right sides together, using a ½-inch seam, stitch cuff piece together at the narrow ends. Fold in half the long way with the bottom open. Turn under and stitch the white ball fringe under the turned seam. Turn under the top of the cuff and stitch.
4. With right sides together, stitch stocking front and back together, leaving the top open for turning. Turn, clip corners and press. Slip cuff piece over the top of the stocking and whipstitch in place. Add a loop for hanging.

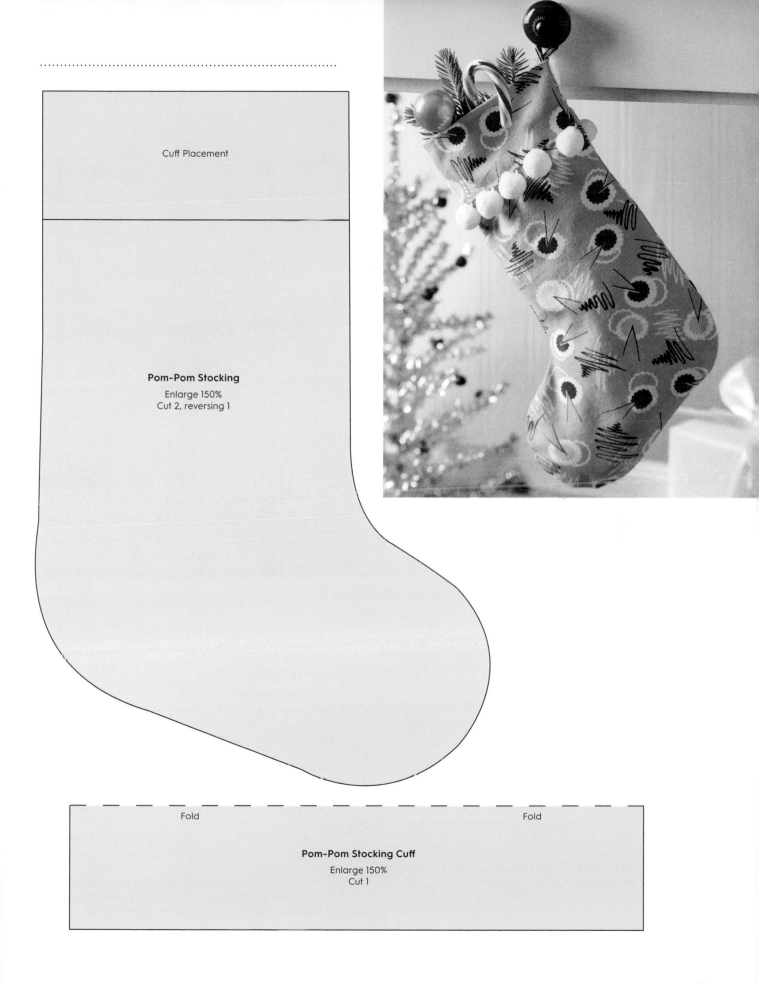

Cuff Placement

Pom-Pom Stocking

Enlarge 150%
Cut 2, reversing 1

Fold

Fold

Pom-Pom Stocking Cuff

Enlarge 150%
Cut 1

SPARKLE WREATH

Simple lines and lots of holiday sparkle make this easy-to-make wreath a bright addition to midcentury holiday decorating.

WHAT YOU NEED

Silver pipe cleaners • Flat wreath form • Scissors • Hot-glue gun and glue sticks • Ribbon for hanging

WHAT YOU DO

1. Lay out pipe cleaners on a flat surface to plan the design. Cut the pipe cleaners in various lengths based on the design. The wreath shown used these lengths: eighty 6-inch pieces, forty 5-inch pieces, forty 4-inch pieces, and sixty 2-inch pieces.

2. Working around the wreath form, attach pipe cleaners using hot glue. Make a base layer and add layers on top of each other until desired look is achieved.

3. Loop a ribbon under the wreath for hanging.

RETRO WRAP

Stamped geometric shapes keep the look crisp and hues of red and green make the pattern oh-so-holiday.

WHAT YOU NEED

Crafts foam pieces • Spray adhesive • Wood block • Brown craft paper • Pencil; ruler • Crafts paint in desired colors • Paper plate • Scissors

WHAT YOU DO

1. Referring to the template, opposite, make a stamp by cutting half circle shapes or other geometric shapes from the foam.

2. Use spray adhesive to attach the foam to the wood block. Let dry.

3. Lay the brown paper on a flat surface. With a pencil and ruler, lightly draw a simple grid on the paper to keep the pattern straight.

4. Put paint on a paper plate then dip the stamp into the paint. Do not use too much paint. Test on a piece of paper first. Stamp onto the brown paper in desired pattern. Let dry.

Retro Wrap Template

RETRO KITCHEN DISPLAY

A vintage sifter with iconic images printed on the side becomes the star of a Christmas centerpiece that reflects the 1950s and '60s. Fill the sifter with fresh greenery and traditional candy canes. Add some frosted cookies and a favorite vintage cookbook and you'll have the perfect holiday display.

PRINTED POINSETTIA PACKAGE TOPPERS

Printed oil cloth was a popular fabric used for tablecloths and place mats in the 1950s. Use this colorful, patterned, and durable fabric to make clever package toppers that say "Merry Christmas!"

WHAT YOU NEED

Oil cloth in desired patterns and colors• Nonwoven felt, such as National Nonwovens • Scissors • Hole punch • Small red pom-poms • Hot-glue gun and glue sticks • Brad clips • Double-stick tape

WHAT YOU DO

1. Enlarge and trace the templates, right. For each poinsettia, cut one large poinsettia from oil cloth and two small poinsettias—one from oil cloth and one from felt.
2. Punch through the center of each shape and secure with a brad clip, layering the pieces.
3. Using hot glue, attach a few small pom-poms to the center of the poinsettia.
4. Use double-stick tape to attach poinsettias to the packages.

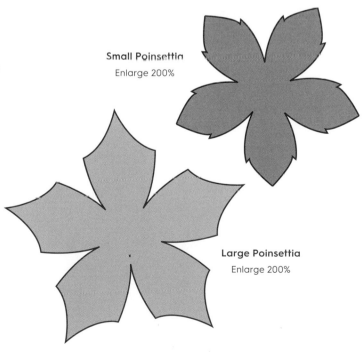

Small Poinsettia
Enlarge 200%

Large Poinsettia
Enlarge 200%

SWEET & SIMPLE MIDCENTURY TRIMS

Rickrack and polka-dots are familiar images from midcentury design. Often used on aprons and other textiles, these trims are ideal for decorating multiple ornaments to hang on an aluminum tree.

WHAT YOU NEED

Clear ball ornaments • Red rickrack • Small red, white, and green dot stickers • Double-stick tape • Fine silver thread

WHAT YOU DO

1. Be sure the ornaments are clean and dry.

2. For the rickrack ornament, measure rickrack and cut a piece just long enough to fit around the ornament. Wrap around and secure with double-stick tape.

3. For the polka-dot ornaments, randomly adhere dots on all sides of the ornament.

4. Place the silver thread through the hanging loop in the ornament.

VINTAGE FABRIC TREES

The 1950s and '60s produced some distinctive fabric-painted tablecloths and tea towels. Bring them back to life in a simple tree shape you can display during the holidays.

WHAT YOU NEED
Vintage tablecloths or tea towels • Iron-on hem tape
• Scissors • Cardboard • Polyester fiberfill

WHAT YOU DO
1. Cut two triangles from each size using the fabric templates, right, or cut two of the same size in desired triangle sizes.
2. On the back of the fabric, iron hem tape onto the two sides of the triangle (not the bottom side.)
3. Attach wrong sides together and iron to create a bond.
4. Cut a slightly smaller triangle from cardboard using the cardboard template, right, and place inside the center of the tree to stabilize.
5. Fill the inside of the triangle with a small amount of polyester fiberfill.

LITTLE ANGELS

Collecting midcentury Christmas items is fun and makes for clean and uncluttered holiday decorating. Display your items to showcase their detail in a simple way. Here, little angels, only 1-inch tall, line up on a tiny doll cupboard.

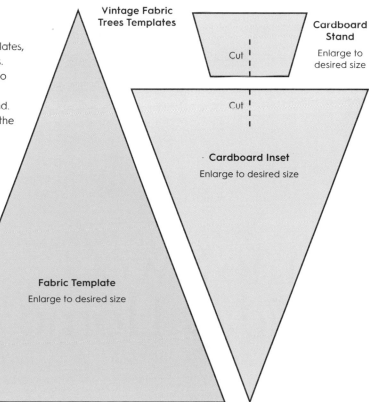

Vintage Fabric Trees Templates

Cardboard Stand
Enlarge to desired size

Cut

Cut

Cardboard Inset
Enlarge to desired size

Fabric Template
Enlarge to desired size

Home Sweet Holiday Home

There is no place like home for the holidays, and this collection of home-inspired projects will fill your house with the Christmas spirit.

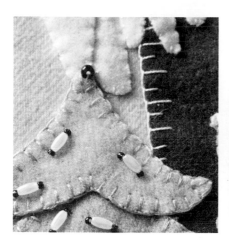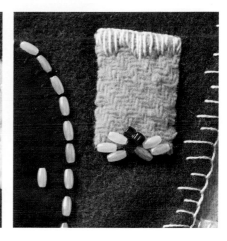

FROSTY MORNING GINGERBREAD HOUSE

Create a masterpiece in fabric when you appliqué this gingerbread house to decorate your holiday home. The elegant piece is beaded and embellished and sure to become a precious heirloom to use year after year.

WHAT YOU NEED

FOR THE BACKGROUND
12×14-inch rectangle light blue/green wool

FOR THE APPLIQUÉ
8×9-inch rectangle rich brown wool for gingerbread house • 8×10-inch rectangle white wool for snow • 8×10-inch rectangle off-white wool for snow • 5×7-inch rectangle hand-dyed light green wool for tree and wreath • 2×3-inch rectangle light teal wool for windows • 2×4-inch rectangle brown plaid wool for chimney • 2×4-inch rectangle red wool for door

FOR THE FREEZER PAPER
18-inch square

FOR THE FUSIBLE WEFT OR FUSIBLE INTERFACING
12×14-inch rectangle

FOR THE BACKING
13×15-inch rectangle coordinating cotton

FOR THE STITCHING AND EMBELLISHING
White, red, green, and light teal size 8 pearl cotton or embroidery floss • White ¼-inch barrel-shape pearl beads (See Sources, page 160) • Red seed and ⅛-inch beads (See Sources, page 160)

WHAT YOU DO

PREPARE THE BACKGROUND AND APPLIQUÉ PIECES
1. Fuse the weft or interfacing to the wrong side of the background.
2. Enlarge and copy the templates, page 64. Trace on the dull side of the freezer paper. Cut out on the traced lines.

3. Referring to the photograph for colors, and the placement diagram, page 65, iron the patterns to the right side of appropriate colors of wool. For the tree, choose a consecutively lighter wool for each section.
4. Cut out around each pattern on the edge of the paper.

STITCHING THE APPLIQUÉ
1. Remove the paper, arrange and pin the house, chimney, and ground snow 1 in place on the background. Position the house with the lower right corner about 2 inches above the lower edge and 2¾ inches in from the right side of the background.
2. Using a blanket stitch, stitch the snow with white pearl cotton or two strands floss. Blanket stitch the sides of house and chimney with white thread using a variety of stitch lengths to give the appearance of bricks. Use a whipstitch on bottom and top edges of house and chimney.
3. Remove the paper, arrange, pin, and stitch door, wreath and windows on house. Blanket stitch edges of wreath and door and whipstitch edges of windows using matching colors of thread. Use a variable length blanket stitch to add snow to the top of the windows.
4. Repeat arranging and stitching ground snow 2, lower roof snow, upper roof snow, and chimney snow in place on the background. Blanket stitch the edges of ground snow and whipstitch the edges of roof and chimney snows.
5. Repeat, arranging and stitching tree 1, 2, and 3 and ground snow 3 in place on the background. Stitch edges with blanket stitch.

FINISH THE PROJECT
1. Lay the stitched wool project on the backing, wrong sides together. Pin in several places. Square up the wool edges while at the same time cutting the backing the same size.
2. Pin around the edges. Using size 8 pearl cotton or three strands floss, blanket stitch around the edges.
3. Using the photograph as inspiration, sew on beads to embellish the gingerbread house.

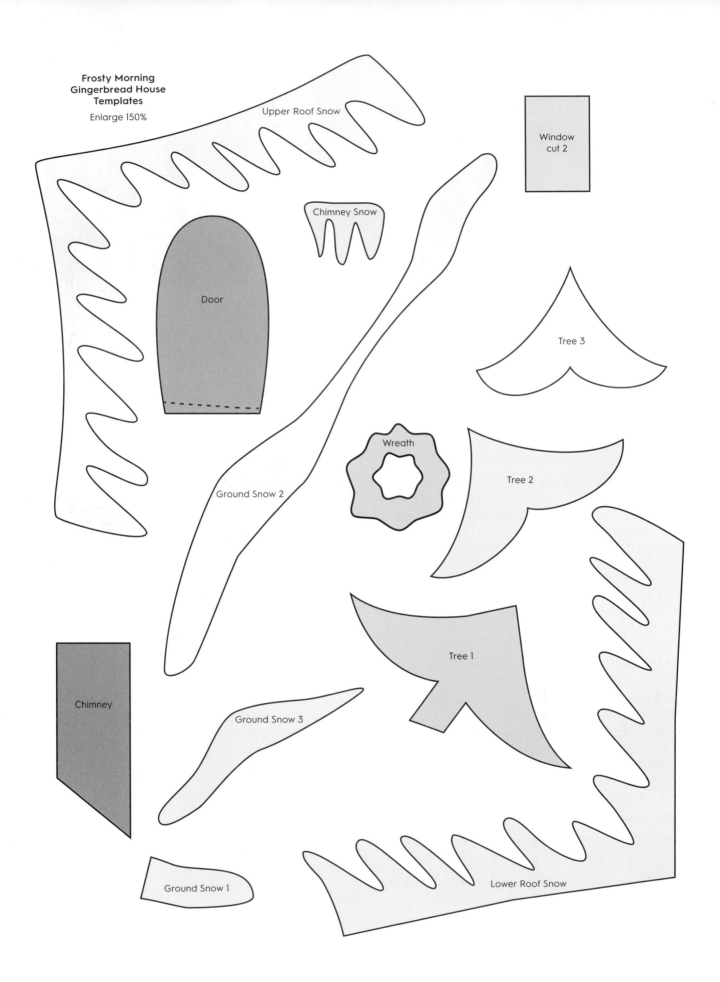

Frosty Morning Gingerbread House Templates

Enlarge 150%

Upper Roof Snow

Window cut 2

Chimney Snow

Door

Tree 3

Wreath

Tree 2

Ground Snow 2

Tree 1

Chimney

Ground Snow 3

Ground Snow 1

Lower Roof Snow

**Frosty Morning
Gingerbread House
Placement Diagram**

Full size

STAMPED PACKAGE WRAP

A humble potato becomes a simple stamp to create a homey little print for holiday gift wrap.

WHAT YOU NEED

Pencil • Paper • Potato • Sharp knife • Paper towels • Acrylic paint in desired color • Foam plate • Plain wrapping paper

WHAT YOU DO

1. Referring to the template, below, draw a house shape on a piece of paper to fit the size of the potato you are using. Use a knife to cut the potato in half, then blot with paper towel to remove moisture.

2. Lay the paper template on the potato half and use a pencil to draw the shape. Carefully cut out the negative space around shape, leaving a stamp shape of a house.

3. Pour a small amount of paint on plate. Dip the potato stamp into the paint and press onto the plain wrapping paper. Do not use too much paint. Let dry.

HOME FOR HOLIDAYS WELCOME

A simple block of wood, a little paint, and printed paper share a lovely thought for Christmas.

WHAT YOU NEED

Wooden block of wood, such as a basswood carving block (available at crafts stores) • Patterned and solid-color scrapbook papers • Decoupage medium, such as Mod Podge • Foam brush • Small wood letters (available at crafts stores) • White spray paint • Scissors

WHAT YOU DO

1. Measure the edges of the wood block and cut the desired print or solid papers to fit.

2. Paint the decoupage medium onto all sides of the block and attach the papers to the block. Brush on top with more decoupage medium. Let dry.

3. Paint the wood letters with spray paint. Let dry. Glue to the front of the block.

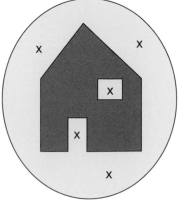

**Stamped Package
Wrap Template**

Cut out X areas

FRIENDLY VILLAGE WREATH

Paper-thin balsa wood is cut and layered to create a tiny village of houses and trees that nestle together to make a welcoming holiday wreath.

WHAT YOU NEED

Floral hoop (10 inch) • Gold spray paint • 1/32-inch-thick strips of balsa wood (available at crafts stores) • Crafts knife, such as X-acto knife • Ruler; cutting board • White crafts paint • Foam paintbrush • Foam adhesive dots • Hot-glue gun and glue sticks • Frosted berries • Cord for hanging

WHAT YOU DO

1. On a covered surface, paint the floral hoop gold. Let dry.
2. Enlarge and copy the templates, below, and transfer to the balsa wood. Cut out using crafts knife. Set aside.
3. Use a pencil to trace around the bottom portion of the floral hoop to create a base pattern. Cut base from balsa wood.
4. Thin the white paint until desired thickness. Brush onto some of the balsa pieces using a foam brush. Let dry.
5. Layer the base, house, and trees, creating depth between layers using foam adhesive dots. Secure the layered pieces on the hoop using hot glue. Let dry.
6. Hot-glue frosted berries to the top of the hoop. Add a string or cord for hanging.

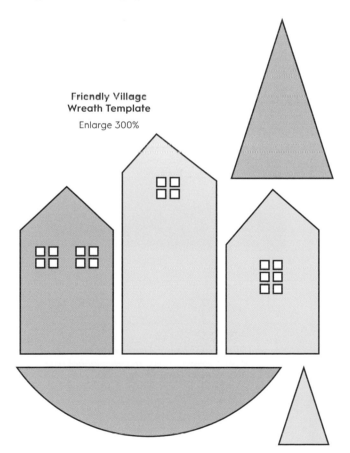

Friendly Village Wreath Template

Enlarge 300%

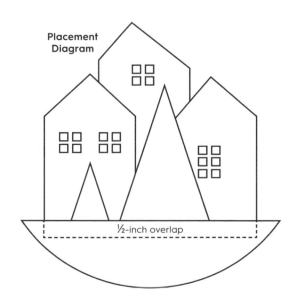

Placement Diagram

½-inch overlap

OH, CHRISTMAS TREE

Build your own little village on a tree by choosing a simple color palette of silver, green, and white. The tiny buildings look like they are perched on snowy hills in an evergreen forest. To start, embellish the tree with sprigs of faux lamb's ears and then layer branches with batting to create snowy hills. Add ornaments such as purchased mercury glass balls and white chipboard snowflakes. Crystal pinecones add a sparkle of new fallen snow. To make the houses, see page 69.

PAPER HOUSE VILLAGE

Purchased papier-mâché houses are dressed up for Christmas with glitter paper, paint, and parchment paper. To give the houses a cheerful glow of a holiday gathering, we glued pieces of parchment paper inside the window openings then lit each house with a flameless, battery-operated votive candle.

WHAT YOU NEED

Papier-mâché houses (available at crafts stores) • Acrylic paint in ivory and green tones • Paintbrush • Glitter paper or glitter and decoupage medium • Crafts glue • Textured scrapbook paper • Scissors • Crafts knife • Flameless votive candles

WHAT YOU DO

1. Paint the papier-mâché house with ivory paint.
2. Paint roofs with medium green paint.
3. Add sparkle by cutting and gluing glitter paper in place. Or brush on decoupage medium, sprinkle glitter, and shake off the excess. Allow to dry and apply a different color of glitter to additional areas.
4. Glue textured paper to the eaves.

5. If desired, lighten the color of trees and evergreen sprigs by submerging each item in diluted bleach briefly, then rinse in water.
6. Cut an opening in the back or bottom of each building using a crafts knife. Insert a flameless votive candle.

SWEET FELTED HOUSE
Little bits of felt are stitched together to make a sweet holiday home to display for Christmas.

WHAT YOU NEED
Tracing paper; pencil • Nonwoven felt, such as National Nonwovens in desired colors • Scissors • Sewing machine • Spray adhesive • Small red pom-pom • Polyester fiberfill

WHAT YOU DO
1. Enlarge and copy the templates, below. Cut two for each house side and front and one of the base.
2. Cut rectangle door, window squares, half circle, and heart from desired colors of felt.
3. Sew side and front pieces together using a ¼-inch seam allowance, with seams on the outside of the house. Attach the half circle, heart, door pieces, and pom-pom doorknob using spray adhesive.
4. Stuff the house lightly with fiberfill and place on the house base. Glue or hand stitch in place.

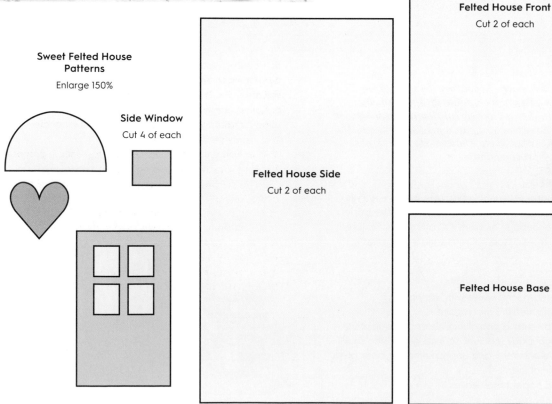

Sweet Felted House Patterns

Enlarge 150%

Side Window

Cut 4 of each

Felted House Side

Cut 2 of each

Felted House Front

Cut 2 of each

Felted House Base

ROW HOUSE PILLOW

Snippets of Christmas fabrics are cut into house shapes and lined up to make a row house pillow that says "Merry Christmas!" The pillow top is strip-pieced first and the shapes are then hand-appliquéd onto the pillow top.

WHAT YOU NEED

Christmas-print fabrics in desired prints and colors • Fusible iron-on webbing stuffing or pillow form • Embroidery floss and needle

WHAT YOU DO

1. Cut ten 3×3½-inch pieces from print fabric. With long sides together and using ¼-inch seams, stitch five pieces together, twice, making two strips. Stitch those strips together making the middle section of the pillow.

2. Cut twenty 1½-inch squares; stitch together in groups of 10, using ¼-inch seam making two strips.

3. Stitch the small-square strips to the top and bottom of the center section. Press.

4. Enlarge and copy the templates, below. Cut the shapes from desired fabrics. Iron webbing to the back of the shapes and fuse onto the stitched section referring to the photograph for placement. Use the blanket stitch to appliqué around each house, moon, and star, placing where desired.

5. Sew borders to pillow top if desired. Finish pillow as desired.

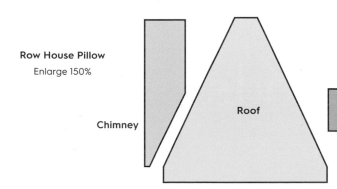

Row House Pillow

Enlarge 150%

Chimney

Roof

Window

Moon

Star

Into the Woods

Natural and fantasy combine with the whorl of
woodgrain, the softness of felt, and the texture
of evergreen to make your holiday an
all-natural experience.

Henry

WOODLAND FRIENDS

Nature-inspired graduated tones of color in nonwoven felt layer together to form sweet little creatures to celebrate the holiday with you.

WHAT YOU NEED

Nonwoven felt, such as National Nonwoven in desired colors • Scissors • Embroidery floss • Spray adhesive • Polyester fiberfill • Needle • Thread to match fabrics • Ribbon

WHAT YOU DO

1. Enlarge, trace, and cut out templates, below. Choose the templates needed for each animal and cut out the shapes from the desired colors of felt.

2. Stitch two small eyes and one small nose using embroidery floss onto body base.

3. Attach body base 2 onto body base 1 or 3 (depending on animal) with spray adhesive. Then layer pieces as listed below.

4. With two strands of embroidery floss, use a running stitch around the edge of the shape to secure front to back, leaving a small opening to stuff with a small amount of polyfill before closing.

5. Stitch a ribbon to the top for hanging.

For the OWL: (Back) Body Base 1, (Front) Ribbon, Body Base 1, Body Base 2, Owl Head, Tail/Wing

For the RACCOON: (Back) Body Base 1, (Front) Ribbon, Ears, Tail/Wing, Raccoon Tail Stripes, Body Base 1, Body Base 2

For the FOX: (Back) Body Base 3, (Front) Ribbon, Ears, Tail/Wing, Fox Tail Stripe, Body Base 3, Body Base 2

Woodland Friends
Enlarge 200%

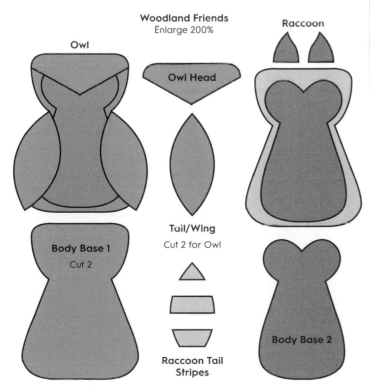

Owl

Owl Head

Tail/Wing
Cut 2 for Owl

Body Base 1
Cut 2

Raccoon Tail
Stripes

Raccoon

Body Base 2

Fox

Ears

Body Base 3
Cut 2

Fox Tail
Stripe

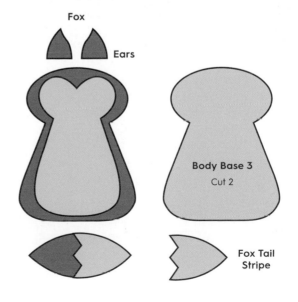

CHUNKY WOODLAND GARLAND

Wood shapes in discs and beads combine to make a natural garland for your evergreen tree.

WHAT YOU NEED

¾-inch wooden beads • Fabric dye, such as Rit • Water • Drill and drill bit • 1½-inch wood discs (available at crafts stores) • Twine or natural string • Scissors

WHAT YOU DO

1. To dye the beads, mix hot water with fabric dye in proportion of about 5 ounces of water to 2 teaspoons of dye. Soak wooden beads in mixture about 30 minutes or longer for richer color. When desired color is achieved, rinse with cold water until water runs clear. Let dry.
2. Using a drill and bit, drill holes through the center of wood disc.
3. Plan the design by laying out the discs and the beads. Thread the discs and beads on the twine or string. Tie a knot at the end and trim the ends.

GLITTERING BIRDS

Purchased bird trims are dressed for the holidays with a touch of paint and a dusting of sparkling glitter.

WHAT YOU NEED

Artificial birds trims, (See Sources, page 160) • Decoupage medium such as Mod Podge • Small paintbrush • Glitter • Crafts paint in desired colors

WHAT YOU DO

1. Plan where you want the glitter and paint to be on the bird.
2. Using paint and paintbrush, coat areas where you want to add color. Let dry.
3. Using decoupage medium, brush small areas of head and wing sections. Dust with glitter. Let dry.

NATURALLY BEAUTIFUL WREATH

A fresh evergreen wreath is adorned with natural beauty and a few little sparkling birds and jingle bells to create a stunning door decor. Wire jingle bells and Glittering Birds and attach to the wreath first. Then tuck in some eucalyptus stems, sticks, and clusters of jingle bells. Tie an oversized bow using two ribbons and wire to the top for the final touch.

TREE DELIVERY

When Santa arrives with the Christmas tree, he's an especially welcome visitor. His cream beard and red garb stand out against the rich midnight-black background. Simple stitching embellishes the wool appliqués, adding depth and dimension.

WHAT YOU NEED

Two 13-inch squares of black wool (pillow front and back) • Fusible web • 15-inch square of red wool (coat, hat) • 3-inch square of desired flesh color wool (face) • 5-inch square of cream wool (beard, mustache, pom-pom) • 5-inch square of taupe wool (hat trim, cuff, eyes) • ¼×6-inch strip of light brown wool (tree trunk) • 3½-inch square of dark brown wool (mitten) • Scraps of black wool (buttons) • Scraps of assorted green wools (tree) • Embroidery floss: black, taupe, ecru, dark brown, teal, red • Embroidery needle • Water- or air-soluble fabric pen • Cosmetic blush • Sewing thread: black • Polyester fiberfill

WHAT YOU DO

CUT FABRICS

1. Enlarge and copy templates, below and on page 80. Lay fusible web, paper side up, over templates. Use a pencil to trace each pattern, with the exception of the coat, the number of times indicated on patterns, leaving ½ inch between tracings. Cut out each fusible-web shape roughly ¼ inch outside traced lines.

2. Following manufacturer's instructions, press each fusible-web shape onto wrong side of designated wool; let cool. Cut out wool shapes on drawn lines. Peel off paper backings. Trace and cut coat from red wool.

APPLIQUÉ AND EMBROIDER PILLOW TOP

1. Refer to page 160 for stitch diagrams. Referring to photo, opposite, align coat with pillow front bottom and side edges; pin along sides. Using two strands of black floss, blanket-stitch top of coat to pillow front.

2. Arrange face, hat, beard, and mustache at top of coat. When pleased with arrangement, remove hat, beard, and mustache. Following manufacturer's instructions, fuse face in place. Fuse hat in place. Blanket-stitch around outside hat edges with black.

3. Fuse hat trim along inside hat edge, covering the edge. Whipstitch edges of trim using one strand of taupe floss. Fuse beard to face and coat. Whipstitch beard edges using one strand of ecru floss. Fuse mustache to beard. Whipstitch mustache edges using one strand of ecru. Fuse pom-pom to hat tip. Whipstitch using two strands of taupe.

4. Referring to photo and overlapping pieces, arrange tree trunk, mitten, cuff, and tree triangles; fuse pieces in place. Whipstitch tree trunk using two strands of dark brown floss. Whipstitch tree triangles using one strand of teal floss.

5. Fuse buttons to coat front. Whipstitch the buttons using two strands of black floss. Stem-stitch letters on tree using two strands of red floss. Referring to photo, add straight stitches and French knots below each tree triangle using two strands of red. Stitch a red French knot at top of tree. Fuse eyes to face. Stitch a French knot in the center of each eye using two strands of black floss. Blanket-stitch mitten using two strands of black floss. Blanket-stitch the cuff using two strands of dark brown floss.

6. Using a fabric pen, mark arm and nose outlines. Stem-stitch arm outlines using two strands of black floss. Straight-stitch nose lines using one strand of black. Straight-stitch mouth using two strands of red.

7. Brush cosmetic blush onto cheeks.

ASSEMBLE PILLOW

1. With right sides together and using a ½-inch seam allowance, sew together pillow front and back; leave a 7-inch opening along the bottom edge. Clip the corners and turn pillow cover right side out.

2. Stuff with polyester fiberfill and hand-sew the opening closed.

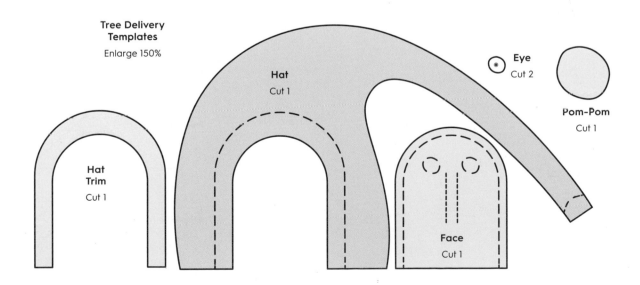

Tree Delivery Templates

Enlarge 150%

Hat Trim — Cut 1
Hat — Cut 1
Eye — Cut 2
Pom-Pom — Cut 1
Face — Cut 1

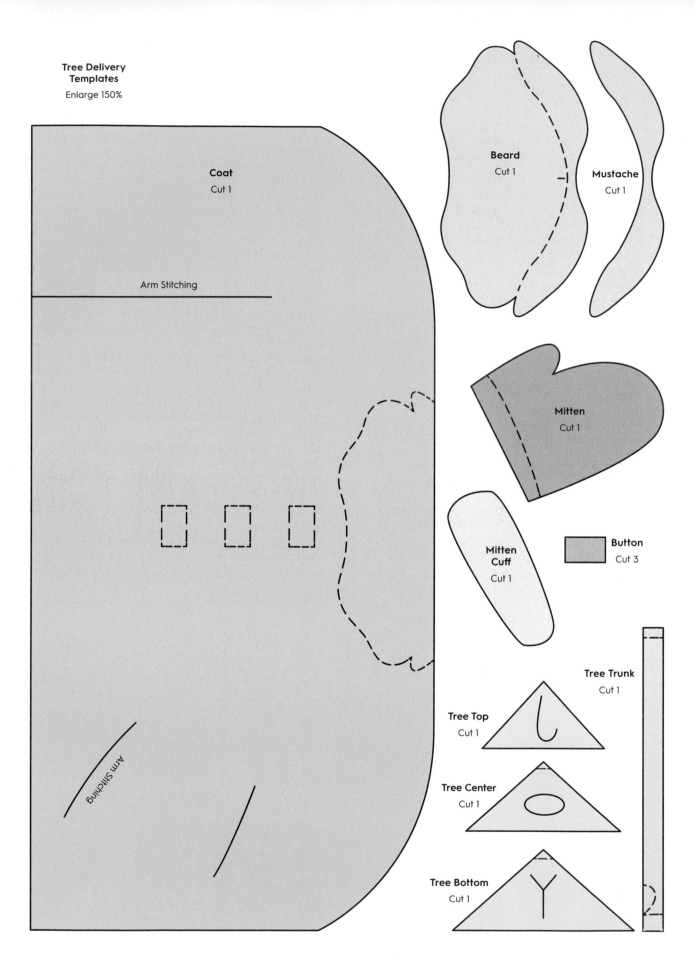

Tree Delivery Templates

Enlarge 150%

Coat
Cut 1

Arm Stitching

Arm Stitching

Beard
Cut 1

Mustache
Cut 1

Mitten
Cut 1

Mitten Cuff
Cut 1

Button
Cut 3

Tree Trunk
Cut 1

Tree Top
Cut 1

Tree Center
Cut 1

Tree Bottom
Cut 1

LOG CABIN TABLE SETTING

Buffalo-check print becomes the inspiration for a colorful holiday table setting. Tuck a wide plaid ribbon under black and red plates and add a matching mug. Choose a linenlike black napkin and tie it up with twine and sticks. Print off each guest's name and glue to a small piece of birch for a name card. Miniature vintage Santas and a vintage miner's light complete the log cabin holiday look.

WOODLAND BIRCH TREE

Little snippets of birch bark overlap to create a lovely textural tree to decorate your mantel or table.

WHAT YOU NEED

Sheets of birch bark, (See Sources, page 160) • Pencil • Foam Christmas tree cone form such as Styrofoam (ours is 12 inches tall) • Hot-glue gun and glue sticks • Scissors

WHAT YOU DO

1. Lay a sheet of birch bark on a flat surface and draw a tear-drop shape near the corner. Cut out the shape and hold it up to the tree form to check scale.

2. When satisfied with the shape, cut tear-drop shapes from the sheets of birch. Cut about 50 pieces, cutting more if needed.

3. Starting at the bottom and working your way around, attach the birch (point towards the top) around the perimeter of the tree form using hot glue. Work your way around until you've reached the top. Let dry.

OVER-THE-RIVER TABLE TOP

A fresh-cut wood slab resting under a plain glass plate sets the stage for a back-to-the woods table setting. A larger slab of wood serves as a tray and a flat rock becomes a surface for a stamped place holder. A clear glass ornament is filled with findings from a walk in the woods—acorns, sticks, bark, and berries.

FOREST-FINDINGS MIRROR

Gather this year's crop of acorns and other forest findings and put them to use by making a beautifully textured mirror frame. Choose a small, simple frame and use crafts glue or hot glue to secure findings in place, overlapping as you glue. Add a cord for hanging.

EVERGREEN-INSPIRED WRAP

Evergreen boughs are the motif that repeats over and over again to create beautiful wrapping paper for those special gifts.

WHAT YOU NEED

Brown craft paper • Evergreen boughs cut into small lengths • Double-stick tape • Spray paint in desired color • Acorns • Twine • Scissors

WHAT YOU DO

1. In a well-ventilated area, lay the craft paper on a covered surface and secure to lay flat. Arrange the evergreen boughs on the paper. Secure temporarily with tape.
2. Spray paint on the boughs. Let dry. Remove the boughs. If the desired look is not yet achieved, lay the boughs on the paper again and spray over the first layer. Let dry.
3. Spray acorns with the same color paint. Let dry.
4. Wrap the package and tie on the acorns with twine.

BACK-COUNTRY PINECONE WREATH

*Create a cabin-ready wreath for the door using a handmade or purchased pinecone
wreath. Spray-paint the wreath white and let dry. Then paint the wreath teal. Let dry.
Tie a bow from plaid flannel and attach at the top of the wreath.*

HOOP WREATH

A basic embroidery hoop is the base for the simple yet stunning wreath. Choose the size of embroidery hoop that you like. Then select decorative accents, faux or fresh, and lay out the cuttings in an arrangement at the top. Loop twine around the cuttings, secure, and tie off. Using twine instead of glue lets you swap out cuttings during the season. Add a loop of twine around the top or a wire for hanging.

FIRED-UP GIFT BAGS

For the outdoor lovers on your Christmas list, keep a stash of gift bags handy for guests. Fill the bag with kindling and add a decorative box of matches. Tie it all up with some holiday greenery and a bright red bow. To make your own decorative matchboxes, use a plain box of matches and cover with holiday scrapbook paper prints. Add a sandpaper strip as a match striker.

INSIDE WONDERLAND

*Create an outdoor winter wonderland no matter what
the climate. Bring the outdoors in with potted lemon
cyprus trees and birch logs in galvanized containers.
Create a display of candles in glass vessels filled with
nonflammable artificial snow. Finish off the look with a
lush fresh wreath and a basket filled with wool socks for
guests who want to curl up and chat awhile.*

SPELL IT OUT

*An oversized chalkboard spells a holiday message for all
to enjoy. Simply frame a large chalkboard in a red frame
or make your own chalkboard look by painting a board
with chalkboard paint. Surround it with plaid pillows,
holiday boots, ice skates, and logs of birch.*

CHUNKY WOOD CANDLES

Rough-cut wood makes perfect holders for tea candles to glow for the holidays.

WHAT YOU NEED
Wood fence posts • Saw • Tea candles in metal liners • Drill and drill bit to fit candle size • Twine • Scissors • Beads

WHAT YOU DO
1. Lay out wood pieces and plan the height you want. Cut to that height.
2. Using the drill, drill straight down through the top of the cut piece. Try the candle in the opening to see if it fits, adjusting as necessary.
3. Thread beads or other embellishments on the twine and wrap around the holders.

Never leave a burning candle unattended.

NATURE SING TABLESCAPE

Create a simple yet stunning tabletop that showcases some of nature's most elegant shapes and textures. Choose a muslin table runner and candles in the color of tree bark. Position the candles randomly down the table center and add fresh apples, eucalyptus, greenery, and unfrosted sugar cookies in the shape of stars.

Never leave a burning candle unattended.

Center of Attention

Make your holiday centerpiece the talk of the table when you create these simply beautiful works of art.

CHRISTMAS PINKS

Soft pink roses and greenery are arranged in a vintage silver sugar bowl for an elegant arrangement for your table. Toss some pink ornaments on the table for the perfect finishing touch.

SILVER AND GOLD

Simple clear glass cake stands are filled with clear and mercury glass ball ornaments and bits of holiday greenery to make a sparkling centerpiece. Simple gold feathers are tucked into the arrangement and a silver bird adds interest.

CHRISTMAS CANDY INSPIRATION

Candy canes and ribbon candy are the inspiration for holiday centerpieces that are Christmas red and white that use all-year flowers for their blooms.

DAISY CHAIN

Long-stemmed Gerbera daisies rest easily in matching glass vases with bits of holly, red ornaments, and ribbon candy adding balance at the base.

CHRISTMAS PAST

A white enamel coffee pot becomes the vase for red and white blooms with just a hint of holiday greenery. A vintage shaker set and candy canes complete the arrangement.

TROPHY WINNER

A poinsettia plant is an inexpensive holiday accessory. For a grand presentation of the humble beauty, carefully snip the showy bracts from the plant and create a gorgeous arrangement. Paired with seeded eucalyptus and red pepper berries in a trophy-shape vase, these cream-and-pink dames make a winning design.

HOLIDAY PLENTY

A tin tray cradles deep-purple candles surrounded by assorted grapes and cherries. Bits of fresh rosemary are tucked among the grapes for a most-aromatic arrangement which rests on a vintage piece of European lace.

Never leave a burning candle unattended.

THE CHRISTMAS ROSE

Christmas-red rose blooms make a table sing with the holiday spirit. Choose a low clear-glass bowl and fill with water. Cut the blooms from red roses and float them in the water. Add some greenery and dust with pink glitter for added sparkle.

FINE FANFARE

Sitting atop stemmed mercury glass vessels, these arrangements include cream-and-green poinsettias, small glass ornaments, and boxwood sprigs. This arrangement would be especially pretty along a mantel. But avoid placing poinsettias above a roaring fire—heat destroys the bracts.

UNDERSTATED

A dozen pastel roses and a vintage enamel pail make an unexpected centerpiece that combines a farmhouse look with delicate beauty. Use enough roses to fill whatever pail you have and cut them so they just peek over the edge. Add some greenery to fill.

ELEGANCE

Antique English china in blue and white showcases pure white hydrangeas with some feathery greenery added for holiday charm. Add a few blue Christmas baubles for a striking holiday centerpiece.

TINY TIM

A "Merry Christmas" tea cup is the vessel to hold petite blooms. You can use any vintage cup and fill it with tiny flowers and greenery. Make this for a sweet centerpiece for a small table or for a much-loved table favor for each guest to take home.

POINSETTIA CHARM

Pink poinsettias rest in a sea of colorful ornaments for a stunning yet simple centerpiece. The ornaments are in a shallow basket and are added after the poinsettias are positioned.

AT FIRST BLUSH

Purchased ornaments in a soft blush color surround a pastel pink candle centered in a clear glass compote. The compote sets on a rose gold tray with more ornaments scattered on the tray. String a few ornaments on ribbon to dangle over the edge of the compote.

Never leave a burning candle unattended.

CITRUS TRIO

Create an aroma of sweet citrus for your holiday table. Choose candles of different heights to set on a cake stand. Then slice lemons, limes, and oranges to surround the candles. Add a citrus-color ornament or two and some greenery if you like.

Never leave a burning candle unattended.

REINDEER GAMES

Little brown votive candles line up to appear to be looking for Santa. Before adding the candles to the votive holders, thread a red bead on some twine and wrap around the center of the holder. Tie to secure. Then use copper wire to form two little antler shapes for each candle. Put the candle in the votive and tuck the wire antlers behind each candle. Line the candles up on a metal tray and add some sticks and pieces of birch.

Never leave a burning candle unattended.

Sweater Sets

Bring out the sweaters...Christmas is almost here! Tired old sweaters get a new spin as holiday decor—no knitting required. Grab your glue gun and deck the halls with these fast and easy-to-make warm fuzzies.

SOFT-AND-SWEET SWEATER STARS

Purchased 3-D paper star shapes are quickly transformed into soft and colorful trims for your holiday decorating.

WHAT YOU NEED

Cardboard star ornaments (available at crafts stores) • Discarded sweaters, flattened and pressed • Scissors • Decoupage medium such as Mod Podge • Foam brush • Hot-glue gun and glue sticks

WHAT YOU DO

1. Lay the cardboard star ornament on an interesting section of the discarded sweater. Cut around the shape, leaving about 1 inch excess all around.

2. Use a foam brush to coat the star with decoupage medium. Starting at the center, press sweater fabric onto the star form and tuck the ends around to the back.

3. If needed, secure with hot glue.

Sewing with Sweaters

Sewing with discarded or well-worn sweaters is a fun way to get the look of a knit item without really knitting it. Choose sweaters with small designs and ribbing to use for edges of mittens and stockings. Wash in cold water and dry before using. Cut into flat pieces and press. To assemble sweater projects you can sew by hand, use a sewing machine, or even assemble with fusible bonding tape. When choosing a sweater to repurpose, the chunkier the knit, the more difficult it is to work with, but it can work well if using as strips. A finer-gauge sweater works well for smoother looks or smaller shapes.

COZY SWEATER WREATH

Strips of a printed sweater wrap around a wreath form for an easy-to-make wreath for your front door.

WHAT YOU NEED

Discarded knitted sweaters, flattened and pressed •
Styrofoam wreath form • Cutting board and rotary cutting
knife • Hot-glue gun and glue sticks • Red grosgrain ribbon

WHAT YOU DO

1. Using a cutting mat and a rotary cutting knife, cut pieces
from the sweater into 6-inch wide strips, cutting on the
diagonal. Fold the cut pieces in half, the long way, so they
become 3 inches wide.
2. Using hot glue, attach the strips around the form,
wrapping the wreath at an angle.
3. If needed, secure with hot glue. Loop a ribbon around
the middle to hang. Attach a sweater star in the center
if desired.

RIBBED SWEATER BOX
Trim a small covered box with scraps of a fun-print sweater for a soft and cozy wrap they will love.

WHAT YOU NEED
Discarded print sweaters, flattened and pressed • Small cardboard box with lid • Scissors • Hot-glue gun and glue sticks • Small piece of ribbon

WHAT YOU DO
1. Lay the box on the sweater pieces and measure, cutting the sweater to fit the sides of the box.
2. Measure and cut for the top, using the ribbing of the sweater for the top edge of the box.
3. Using hot glue, attach the pieces to the box.
4. Make a bow from the scraps and glue a small piece of ribbon around the piece. Glue to the top of the box.

SIMPLE SWEATER STOCKINGS

Quick for you to make, and for Santa to fill, these soft stockings are perfect for holding Christmas treasures.

WHAT YOU NEED

Discarded sweaters, flattened and pressed • Scissors • Hot-glue gun and glue sticks • Small piece of yarn

WHAT YOU DO

1. Enlarge the template, right. Choose the section of the sweater to be used. Lay the sweater pieces right sides together with ribbing at the top. Place the template on the sweater fabric so the ribbing is at the top. Trace around the template and cut out leaving a ¼-inch seam allowance.

2. Pin sides and sew around the stocking using zigzag stitch, leaving the top open. Trim off excess around the seams. Turn right side out. Turn cuff over.

3. For a hanger, form a loop of yarn and sew it into place at the stocking opening at the cuff.

Ribbing

Simple Sweater Stockings Template

Enlarge 200%

VOTIVE WRAP

Create an adorable votive wrap using the cuff of a sweater. Simply fit the arm of the sweater around a votive or vase and cut off the ends about 2 inches longer than your vessel. Fold under the ends and hot-glue in place. Trim with bells or ribbons if desired. Slip sweater over the base.

Never leave a burning candle unattended.

SOFT MINI TREE TABLETOP

Plant a mini grove of sweater trees on a tabletop or mantel by transforming Christmas-red sweaters into holiday cheer.

WHAT YOU NEED

Discarded red-print sweaters, flattened and pressed • Scissors • Polyester fiberfill • ¼-inch wooden dowel • Hot-glue gun and glue sticks • Drill and drill bit • Natural wood disc (available at crafts stores)

WHAT YOU DO

1. Choose the section of the sweater to be used. Choose the size template you want and enlarge. Lay the sweater pieces right sides together. Trace around the template and cut out.
2. Pin sides and sew, leaving a small gap in the center of the base of the tree form. Turn right side out, stuff with fiberfill, and insert the top of the wooden dowel into the triangle. Glue shut to finish.
3. Drill a hole in the center of a natural wood disc and insert dowel.

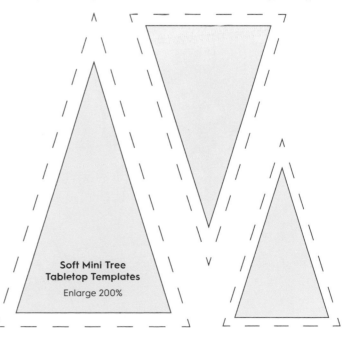

Soft Mini Tree Tabletop Templates

Enlarge 200%

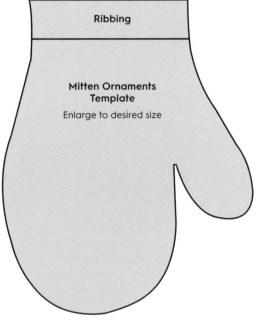

Ribbing

**Mitten Ornaments
Template**

Enlarge to desired size

Graphic Star Garland
Pattern

MITTEN ORNAMENTS

Make these cute mitten ornaments by cutting out simple mitten shapes from a patterned sweater. Use a bit of interfacing to give the mittens lasting shape.

WHAT YOU NEED
Discarded sweaters, flattened and pressed • Scissors • Fusible interfacing • Iron • Hot-glue gun and glue sticks • Small piece of yarn

WHAT YOU DO
1. Enlarge the template, opposite, to desired size or make your own template. Trace around the mitten template and cut out adding a ¼-inch seam allowance. Lay the sweater pieces right sides together with the ribbing of sweater at the top. Lay the template on the sweater pieces with ribbing at the top and cut out. Fuse interfacing to the inside of one side of one of the mitten pieces.
2. With right sides together, pin sides and sew around the mitten using a zigzag stitch, leaving the top open. Trim off excess around the seams. Turn right side out.
3. For a hanger, form a loop of yarn and sew it into place at the top opening.

GRAPHIC STAR GARLAND

This graphic star garland is made by cutting star shapes from fine-gauge sweater fabric. Use the template, above, or create your own star shape. Adhere heavy iron-on fusible interfacing to the backs of the stars and trim. Hot-glue a large sequin in the center of each star for a touch of twinkle. Glue the stars to yarn and hang.

SWEATER PILLOWS

A pillow cover made from the midsection of an outgrown sweater is just the touch for a cozy corner. To make it, buy a pillow insert that fits snugly in the torso of the sweater. Turn the sweater inside out and insert the pillow to make the appropriate length to cut the sweater. Remove the insert and stitch across the bottom edge of the sweater. Trim off the top part of the sweater and turn the sweater right side out. Insert the pillow form and whipstitch the pillow closed.

EMBROIDERY HOOP TRIMS

Use 3-inch diameter hoops (available at crafts stores) and patterned cutouts from worn-out winter sweaters. Place the hoops over display-worthy areas of a sweater and tighten. Trim the excess material. If you like, arrange in a tree pattern and use removable adhesive to attach to the wall.

Christmas Eve Soup Supper

Celebrate coziness and comfort with a casual Christmas Eve meal of soup, salad, and bread. A variety of flavor profiles and preparation methods lets you choose the combination that's best for you and yours.

BEEFY TEXAS CHILI

The finely crushed tortilla chips or masa harina stirred in at the end of the cooking time helps to thicken the chili just slightly and give it a bit of body.

WHAT YOU NEED

3   Tbsp. vegetable oil
2½ to 3 lb. boneless beef chuck pot roast, trimmed of fat
     and cut into ½-inch cubes*
     Black pepper
1½ cups chopped onions
4   cloves garlic, minced
1   Tbsp. ground cumin
1½ to 2 tsp. ancho chile powder
4   cups reduced-sodium beef broth
1   14.5-oz. can diced tomatoes, undrained
1   8-oz. can tomato sauce
1   to 2 canned chipotle peppers in adobo sauce, finely
     chopped

3   Tbsp. very finely crushed tortilla chips or masa harina
     Toppings, such as sour cream, snipped fresh cilantro,
     sliced fresh jalapeño chile peppers (tip, page 124),
     and/or shredded cheddar cheese

WHAT YOU DO

1. In a 4- to 5-quart pot heat 1 Tbsp. oil over medium-high heat. Sprinkle meat with pepper. Add one-third of the meat to the pot; cook until browned. Remove meat from pot, draining off liquid. Repeat twice with remaining oil and meat.
2. Add onions and garlic to the same pot (add additional oil if needed). Cook and stir 4 minutes or until tender. Add cumin and ancho chile powder; cook and stir 1 minute more.
3. Return meat to pot. Add the next four ingredients (through chipotle peppers). Bring to boiling; reduce heat. Simmer, covered, 1 hour, stirring occasionally. Uncover and simmer 1 hour more or until beef is tender and chili is slightly thickened, stirring occasionally.
4. Slowly add crushed chips to the chili, stirring constantly to incorporate. Simmer 5 minutes. Serve with toppings. Makes 4 to 6 servings.
*Tip If you prefer, use ground beef chuck instead of the roast.

CHEESEBURGER SOUP

If you have kids in your crowd (or even if you don't!), this whimsical soup is sure to be a hit.

WHAT YOU NEED

1	lb. ground beef
½	cup chopped onion
½	cup chopped celery
2	cloves garlic, minced
2	Tbsp. all-purpose flour
2	14.5-oz. cans low-sodium beef broth
2	medium potatoes, coarsely chopped
1	14.5-oz. can diced tomatoes, drained
8	oz. American cheese slices, torn
1	6-oz. can tomato paste
¼	cup ketchup
2	Tbsp. Dijon mustard
1	cup whole milk
6	cocktail buns, split and toasted*
	Assorted condiments (pickles, onions, lettuce, mustard, and/or ketchup) (optional)
	Hot french fries (optional)

WHAT YOU DO

1. In a large pot cook beef, onion, celery, and garlic over medium heat until meat is browned and vegetables are tender. Drain fat. Sprinkle flour over beef mixture; cook and stir 2 minutes. Stir in broth and potatoes. Bring to boiling, stirring occasionally; reduce heat. Simmer, covered, 10 minutes or until potatoes are tender.

2. Stir in tomatoes, cheese, tomato paste, ketchup, and mustard. Cook and stir until cheese is melted and soup comes to a gentle boil. Stir in milk; heat through. Top toasted buns with condiments and serve with soup. If desired, top soup with hot french fries. Makes 6 servings.

*Note To toast buns, preheat the broiler. Place split buns, cut sides up, on a broiler pan. Brush lightly with 1 Tbsp. melted butter or olive oil. Broil, 3 to 4 inches from heat, 1 minute or until lightly toasted.

PORK STEW WITH GREMOLATA

This elegant Italian-inspired stew can be made in a slow cooker or pressure cooker, giving you the flexibility to make it by the best method for your schedule. (Pictured on page 120.)

WHAT YOU NEED

1½	lb. boneless pork shoulder roast, trimmed of fat and cut into 1-inch pieces
1	Tbsp. olive oil
1	14.5-oz. can diced tomatoes, undrained
1	14.5-oz. can beef broth
1	large onion, cut into thin wedges
1	cup sliced carrots
½	cup sliced celery

½	cup dry white wine
2	cloves garlic, minced
¼	tsp. dried thyme, crushed
¼	tsp. salt
⅛	tsp. black pepper
1	Tbsp. butter, softened (pressure cooker only)
1	Tbsp. all-purpose flour (pressure cooker only)
1	Tbsp. quick-cooking tapioca (slow cooker only)
2	cups hot cooked orzo pasta (rosamarina) or rice
1	recipe Gremolata

WHAT YOU DO

1. In a large skillet brown meat, half at a time, in hot oil over medium heat. Drain off fat. Transfer meat to a 3½- or 4-quart slow cooker. Stir in the next 10 ingredients (through pepper) and 1 Tbsp. tapioca, crushed.

2. Cover and cook on low 7 to 8 hours or on high 3½ to 4 hours. Serve as directed. Serve stew over hot cooked orzo and top with Gremolata. Makes 4 servings.

Pressure Cooker Method In a 4- to 6-quart electric pressure cooker use the sauté setting to cook meat, half at a time, in hot oil over medium high heat until browned. Drain off fat. Stir in the next 10 ingredients (through pepper). Lock lid in place. Cook on high pressure 10 minutes. Let stand 15 minutes to release pressure naturally. Release any remaining pressure. Open lid carefully. In a small bowl combine butter and flour; whisk into stew. Cook over medium heat until slightly thickened and bubbly. Serve stew over hot cooked orzo and top with Gremolata.

Gremolata In a small bowl combine ¼ cup snipped fresh Italian parsley, 2 tsp. lemon zest, and 4 cloves garlic, minced.

CURRIED CHICKEN STEW

This slow-cooker stew will fill your house with the amazing aroma of garlic, curry, and cinnamon as it simmers away on the countertop.

WHAT YOU NEED

1¼ lb. skinless, boneless chicken thighs
¾ cup chopped red sweet pepper
¾ cup chopped yellow sweet pepper
1 small onion, sliced
1 jalapeño,* seeded and finely chopped
2 cloves garlic, minced
1 cup low-sodium chicken broth
½ cup golden raisins
½ cup shredded coconut
3 Tbsp. curry powder
1 tsp. salt
¼ tsp. ground cinnamon
¼ tsp. cayenne pepper (optional)
½ cup unsweetened coconut milk
1 Tbsp. cornstarch
2 cups hot cooked rice (optional)
¾ cup lightly salted cashews, coarsely chopped

WHAT YOU DO

1. In a 3½- or 4-quart slow cooker combine chicken, sweet peppers, onion, jalapeño, and garlic. Stir in broth, raisins, coconut, curry powder, salt, cinnamon, and, if desired, cayenne pepper.
2. Cover and cook on low 8½ to 9 hours or on high 4 to 4½ hours.

3. If using low-heat setting, turn to high-heat setting. In a small bowl stir coconut milk into cornstarch until smooth; stir into slow cooker. Cover and cook 15 to 20 minutes more or until slightly thickened.
4. If desired, serve stew over hot cooked rice. Sprinkle with cashews. Makes 4 servings.
*Tip Chile peppers contain oils that can irritate your skin and eyes. Wear plastic or rubber gloves when working with them.

MANHATTAN CLAM CHOWDER

This brothy and light tomato-based chowder pairs beautifully with Potato-Bacon Batter Bread with Caramelized Onions (page 128).

WHAT YOU NEED

1 pint shucked clams or two 6.5-oz. cans minced clams
1 cup chopped celery
⅓ cup chopped onion
¼ cup chopped carrot
2 Tbsp. olive oil or vegetable oil
1 8-oz. bottle clam juice or 1 cup chicken broth
2 cups cubed red potatoes
1 tsp. dried thyme, crushed
⅛ tsp. cayenne pepper
⅛ tsp. black pepper
1 14½-oz. can diced tomatoes, undrained
2 Tbsp. purchased cooked bacon pieces or cooked crumbled bacon*

WHAT YOU DO

1. Chop fresh clams (if using), reserving juice; set clams aside. Strain clam juice to remove bits of shell. (Or drain canned clams, reserving the juice.) If necessary, add enough water to the reserved clam juice to equal 1½ cups. Set clam juice aside.

2. In a large saucepan cook celery, onion, and carrot in hot oil until tender. Stir in reserved 1½ cups clam juice and the 8 oz. clam juice. Stir in potatoes, thyme, cayenne pepper, and black pepper. Bring to boiling; reduce heat. Simmer, covered, 10 minutes. Stir in undrained tomatoes, clams, and bacon. Return to boiling; reduce heat. Cook 1 to 2 minutes or until heated through. Makes 4 servings.

*Tip If cooking bacon, cook two slices, reserving 2 Tbsp. drippings. Omit oil. Cook celery, onion, and carrot in reserved drippings.

CORN CHOWDER

Creamy and a little sweet, this potato-and-corn chowder is always a crowd-pleaser.

WHAT YOU NEED

1	Tbsp. vegetable oil
1	cup finely chopped carrots
½	cup finely chopped celery
⅓	cup finely chopped onion
3	cups peeled and cubed russet potatoes (about 1 lb.)
3	cups reduced-sodium chicken broth
1	bay leaf
¾	tsp. salt
¾	tsp. dried thyme, crushed
⅛	tsp. paprika
4	cups frozen whole kernel corn
2	cups milk
3	Tbsp. cornstarch
2	Tbsp. dry white wine
1	Tbsp. snipped fresh thyme
4	slices bacon, crisp-cooked and crumbled (optional)
	Cracked black pepper

WHAT YOU DO

1. In a medium saucepan heat oil over medium-high heat. Add carrots, celery, and onion; cook 7 minutes or until tender, stirring occasionally. Transfer to a 4- to 6-quart slow cooker. Stir in potatoes, broth, bay leaf, salt, thyme, and paprika.

2. Cover and cook on low 3 hours or on high 1½ hours or until potatoes are tender. Stir in corn and milk. Cover and cook 1 hour or until heated through.

3. In a small bowl stir together cornstarch and wine; stir into mixture in cooker. Cover and cook 10 minutes more. Stir in fresh thyme.

4. Using a potato masher, gently mash potatoes until soup is slightly thickened. Sprinkle servings with bacon (if using) and pepper. Makes 6 servings.

MOROCCAN RED LENTIL SOUP

If you're looking for a light meal amidst all of the rich holiday fare, this is your soup. It's also meatless, should there be vegetarians in your crowd.

WHAT YOU NEED

2	Tbsp. olive oil
1	cup finely chopped yellow onion
2	Tbsp. finely chopped fresh ginger
2	garlic cloves, minced
1	tsp. ras el hanout
½	tsp. Aleppo pepper
6	cups vegetable broth
2	cups water
2	cups red lentils, rinsed and drained
1½	cups chopped roma tomatoes
	Salt and black pepper
	Plain yogurt
	Fresh cilantro

WHAT YOU DO

1. In a 5- to 6-quart Dutch oven heat oil over medium. Add onion, ginger, and garlic; cook 8 minutes or until softened, stirring occasionally. Stir in ras el hanout and Aleppo pepper; cook 1 minute or until fragrant. Add broth, water, lentils, and tomatoes.

2. Bring to boiling; reduce heat. Simmer, covered, 25 minutes or until lentils are tender, stirring occasionally. Season to taste with salt and pepper. Top servings with yogurt, cilantro, and additional Aleppo pepper. Makes 8 servings.

*Tip If desired, omit fresh tomatoes and use one 14.5-oz. can petite diced tomatoes, undrained, and reduce the water to 1½ cups.

WARM ROASTED BARLEY, KALE, AND APPLE SALAD

You can use either curly-leaf or lacinato kale (also called Tuscan kale or dinosaur kale) in this hearty warm salad.

WHAT YOU NEED

1¼	cups regular pearled barley
¼	cup olive oil
1	tsp. salt
1¼	cups apple cider
¾	cup water
6	cups torn kale leaves
⅓	cup snipped pitted whole dates
2	Tbsp. orange juice
2	Tbsp. cider vinegar
1	cup thinly sliced Braeburn or Honeycrisp apple
⅓	cup crumbed ricotta salata or feta cheese
¼	cup pistachio nuts or toasted walnuts, coarsely chopped

WHAT YOU DO

1. Preheat oven to 375°F. In a 2- to 3-quart casserole combine barley, 1 Tbsp. oil, and salt. Roast, uncovered, 25 minutes or until well toasted, stirring occasionally.

2. Meanwhile, in a small saucepan bring cider and water to boiling. Pour over toasted barley. Roast, covered, 40 minutes or just until barley is tender. Stir in kale, dates, and orange juice. Roast, uncovered, 6 minutes more or until kale begins to soften. Stir in vinegar and remaining oil.

3. Top barley salad with apple slices, ricotta salata, and nuts. Makes 4 servings.

CARAMELIZED SQUASH SALAD WITH PISTACHIOS AND GOAT CHEESE

The pleasant bitterness of the radicchio offers a nice balance to the sweetness of the roasted squash in this colorful salad.

WHAT YOU NEED

1	cup orange juice
3	Tbsp. pure maple syrup
1½	Tbsp. Dijon mustard
1	Tbsp. grated fresh ginger
1½	lb. butternut squash, peeled, seeded, halved crosswise, and cut into ½-inch-wide strips
	Nonstick cooking spray
½	tsp. salt
¼	tsp. black pepper
⅓	cup olive oil
6	cups mixed salad greens
1	small head radicchio, cored and thinly sliced
½	cup roasted salted pistachio nuts
3	oz. goat cheese, crumbled (optional)

WHAT YOU DO

1. For marinade, in a bowl stir together orange juice, maple syrup, mustard, and ginger; set aside ½ cup. Place butternut squash pieces in a large resealable plastic bag set in a shallow dish. Pour remaining marinade over squash. Seal bag; turn to coat squash. Marinate in the refrigerator 1 to 4 hours, turning bag occasionally.

2. Preheat oven to 400°F. Coat a large baking sheet with cooking spray. Drain and discard marinade from squash. Place squash on prepared baking sheet. Roast 26 to 30 minutes or until tender and light brown in spots.

3. For dressing, in a small bowl whisk together the reserved marinade, salt, and pepper. Slowly whisk in the oil. Drizzle 2 to 3 Tbsp. dressing over warm squash; toss to combine. In a large bowl combine the mixed greens, radicchio, and half the pistachios. Toss with half the dressing. Gently toss roasted squash into salad. Top with remaining pistachios and goat cheese. Pass remaining dressing. Makes 6 servings.

WILTED SPINACH SALAD WITH PEARS AND CRANBERRIES

Christmas colors and the wintry flavors of pears and cranberries make this salad an especially festive addition to a holiday meal.

WHAT YOU NEED

2	medium pears, cored and thinly sliced
2	Tbsp. lemon juice
12	cups packaged fresh baby spinach or torn spinach (12 oz.)
¾	cup thinly sliced red onion
	Dash ground black pepper (optional)
4	slices bacon
	Vegetable oil (optional)
½	cup dried cranberries
⅓	cup red wine vinegar
1	Tbsp. sugar
½	tsp. dry mustard
	Gorgonzola cheese, crumbled (optional)

WHAT YOU DO

1. Place pears in a bowl; drizzle with lemon juice. Fill bowl with enough water to cover pears. Place a small plate over pears to submerge pears; set aside. In a large bowl combine spinach and red onion. If desired, sprinkle with pepper; set aside.

2. For dressing, in a Dutch oven cook bacon until crisp. Remove bacon, reserving ¼ cup drippings in Dutch oven. (If necessary, add enough oil to equal ¼ cup). Crumble bacon; set aside. Stir the ½ cup cranberries, the vinegar, sugar, and mustard into drippings in Dutch oven. Bring to boiling; remove from heat. Add spinach mixture. Toss mixture in skillet 30 to 60 seconds or just until spinach is wilted.

3. Transfer spinach mixture to a large bowl. Add bacon; toss to combine. Divide spinach mixture among six salad plates; drain pears and arrange on spinach mixture. If desired, sprinkle with Gorgonzola cheese and additional cranberries. Makes 6 servings.

POTATO-BACON BATTER BREAD WITH CARAMELIZED ONIONS

Mashed potatoes make the texture of this savory bread tender, airy, and moist. Serve it with softened butter or coarse-grain mustard, if you'd like. (Pictured on page 121.)

WHAT YOU NEED

6	slices bacon, chopped
	Cornmeal
½	cup chopped onion
1	cup warm milk (105°F to 115°F)
1	pkg. active dry yeast
⅓	cup butter, melted
1	egg
1	tsp. salt
3	cups all-purpose flour
1	cup leftover or prepared mashed potatoes,* room temperature

WHAT YOU DO

1. In a large skillet cook bacon over medium heat until crisp. Drain bacon on paper towels, reserving ¼ cup drippings in skillet. Brush bottom and sides of an 11×7-inch or 8×8-inch baking pan with 2 Tbsp. reserved drippings; sprinkle generously with cornmeal.

2. Add onion to remaining reserved drippings in skillet; cook over medium heat 6 minutes or until dark brown, stirring occasionally.

3. In a large bowl combine milk and yeast; let stand until foamy. Add butter, egg, salt, and 1 cup flour. Beat with a mixer on medium 2 minutes, scraping bowl as needed. Stir in bacon, onion, the remaining 2 cups flour, and mashed potatoes (dough will be soft and sticky).

4. Transfer dough to prepared baking pan. Cover and let rise in a warm place until double in size (about 40 minutes).

5. Preheat oven to 375°F. Bake 45 to 50 minutes or until golden. Cool in pan on a wire rack 10 minutes. Serve warm or cool on wire rack. Makes 8 servings.

*Tip For prepared mashed potatoes, peel and quarter two small russet potatoes. In a small covered saucepan cook potatoes in lightly salted boiling water to cover 15 to 20 minutes or until very tender. Drain and mash potatoes; measure 1 cup.

EASY SESAME DINNER ROLLS

Fresh-from-the-oven dinner rolls could not be simpler. Start with a loaf of thawed purchased bread dough, then simply shape, coat with a savory mixture of sesame seeds, cornmeal, Parmesan cheese, and lemon-pepper seasoning, and bake.

WHAT YOU NEED

1   16-oz. loaf frozen white or wheat bread dough
¼   cup sesame seeds
2   Tbsp. yellow cornmeal
2   Tbsp. grated Parmesan cheese
1   tsp. salt-free lemon-pepper seasoning
3   Tbsp. butter, melted

WHAT YOU DO

1. Thaw dough according to package directions. Grease a 9×9-inch baking pan; set aside. In a shallow dish or small bowl stir together sesame seeds, cornmeal, Parmesan cheese, and lemon-pepper seasoning. Place butter in a second dish. Cut dough into 16 equal pieces. Shape each piece into a ball by pulling and pinching dough underneath. Roll dough pieces in butter, then sesame seed mixture to lightly coat. Arrange dough pieces, smooth sides up, in the prepared pan.

2. Cover pan with waxed paper. Let rise in a warm place until nearly double in size (45 to 60 minutes).

3. Preheat oven to 375°F. Bake 25 minutes or until golden brown. Transfer rolls to a wire rack. Cool slightly before serving. Makes 16 servings.

Garlic-Herb Rolls Prepare as directed except omit lemon-pepper seasoning and add 1 tsp. dried Italian seasoning, crushed, and ½ tsp. garlic powder to sesame seed mixture.

NO-KNEAD SKILLET FOCACCIA

Baking this flatbread in a cast-iron skillet gives it a delightfully crunchy crust while retaining a tender, chewy center.

WHAT YOU NEED

3   cups all-purpose flour
¾   cup whole wheat or all-purpose flour
1¾   tsp. kosher salt
½   tsp. active dry yeast
1½   cups warm water (120°F to 130°F)
¼   cup chopped pitted Kalamata olives
¼   cup chopped roasted red bell pepper
2   tsp. fresh rosemary or thyme leaves
2   cloves garlic, sliced
2   Tbsp. olive oil

WHAT YOU DO

1. In a large bowl stir together 2 cups all-purpose flour, the whole wheat flour, 1½ tsp. salt, and the yeast. Stir in warm water until mixture is moistened (dough will be sticky and soft). Cover bowl loosely with plastic wrap; let rest at room temperature 2 hours.

2. Lightly grease a 12-inch cast-iron skillet. Using a fork, stir remaining 1 cup all-purpose flour into dough. Gather dough with your hands and spread slightly in prepared skillet. Cover loosely with lightly greased plastic wrap. Let rise at room temperature until puffy (1¾ to 2 hours).

3. Preheat oven to 400°F. Sprinkle dough with olives, roasted pepper, rosemary, and garlic. Drizzle with 1 Tbsp. oil and sprinkle with remaining ¼ tsp. salt. Cook over medium-high heat 3 minutes. Transfer to oven and bake 30 minutes or until golden. Cool slightly in skillet on a wire rack. Drizzle with remaining 1 Tbsp. oil. Serve warm. Makes 10 to 12 servings.

EVERYTHING CRACKER CRISPS

Love everything bagels but want less bread? These pleasingly irregular crisps are the perfect solution.

WHAT YOU NEED

¼   cup sesame seeds
¼   cup poppy seeds
2   Tbsp. dried minced garlic, crushed
2   Tbsp. dried minced onion, crushed
1¼   cups all-purpose flour
1   cup whole wheat flour
1½   tsp. baking powder
1½   tsp. salt
3   Tbsp. vegetable oil
¾   cup plus 3 Tbsp. water

WHAT YOU DO

1. In a small dry skillet stir sesame and poppy seeds over medium heat 1 to 2 minutes or until toasted. Remove from heat. Stir in garlic and onion; cool.

2. In a large bowl combine flours, baking powder, and salt; stir in seed mixture and oil. Add water; stir just until

moistened. Turn dough out onto a lightly floured surface; knead five times or until smooth. Divide dough into eight portions. Cover and let rest 30 minutes.

3. Preheat oven to 450°F. Line a baking sheet with parchment paper. Roll one portion of dough at a time into an 11×5-inch rectangle; transfer to prepared baking sheet. Bake 8 minutes or until brown and crisp, turning once halfway through. Transfer to a wire rack to cool. Break into crackers. Store at room temperature up to 5 days. Makes 36 servings.

A Simpler Season

No worries, no rush! Christmas is almost here but you have plenty of time to create these easy-to-make projects just in the nick of time

CHRISTMAS CHEER

Jingle all the way with oversized jingle bells that form an ombre color garland to hang on your tree or dangle from a newel post. Any color theme will work—just go from light to dark or shade to shade in the same color hue. The results are stunning!

SPARKLING OMBRE BELL GARLAND

Jingle bells sing with the season when they are painted with shades of paint and dusted with glitter.

WHAT YOU NEED

Large jingle bells • Crafts glue • Paintbrush • Fine glitter in desired colors from light to dark • 2 jars or glasses • Sturdy wire • Fine ribbon

WHAT YOU NEED

1. Set up a drying station before you begin by putting two jars a few inches apart. Thread wire through the first bell.
2. Paint the crafts glue on the bell and dust with glitter. Let dry.
3. Prop the bell between the jars to dry adjusting the wire if necessary.
4. Repeat using varying shades of glitter for the other bells. Let dry.
5. Thread the bells on the ribbon for hanging.

CUT-OUT CANDLE WRAPS

A purchased lace-edge paper punch makes quick work of cutting paper lace to decorate your holiday votives.

WHAT YOU NEED

Purchased candles • Cardstock • Lace edge paper punch • Tape or hot-glue gun and glue sticks • Fine gold ribbon

WHAT YOU NEED

1. Create designs on a strip of cardstock using a lace edge paper punch.
2. Wrap around the candle and secure with tape or hot glue.
3. Tie a fine gold ribbon around the top of the votive.

Never leave a burning candle unattended

Bright Christmas ribbons and clear ball ornaments quickly transform into elegant trimmings for your holiday home.

GATHERED RIBBON WRAP

Layers of ribbon are stitched together to make a stunning package ribbon or festive garland.

WHAT YOU NEED
Wide and narrow ribbon: (we used 4-inch and 2½-wide satin ribbon) • Embroidery floss in desired color • Needle • Scissors

WHAT YOU DO
1. Layer the two ribbons atop each other on a flat surface.
2. With the needle and floss, attach the two ribbons together using a running stitch down the center. Gather ribbon to create bunting.

SPARKLING CLEAR TRIMS

Choose sparkling by-the-yard trims from your fabric store and create these one-of-a-kind trims in a matter of minutes. Simply cut the length you need to wrap around a clear ball and hot-glue or tape in place. Display on a tree or in a pretty bowl.

SCRAPPY GIFT BOXES

Purchased gift boxes are decorated with contrasting printed scrapbook paper and white glitter jingle bells for a simple and stunning presentation.

WHAT YOU NEED

Cardboard gift boxes • Scissors • Scrapbook or handmade paper in small-print patterns• Decoupage medium, such as Mod Podge • Foam paintbrush • Ribbon • Jingle bells

WHAT YOU DO

1. Measure and cut the decorative paper to fit the sides and top of the box to be covered.
2. Lay the box on a covered surface and coat the outside of the gift box with decoupage medium using a foam brush.
3. Attach the cut paper to the box. Let dry.
4. Thread a jingle bell on the ribbon and attach to the box.

OH-THE-JOY CARDS

Spell out holiday cheer with two simple ways to make holiday cards in a jiffy.

FOR THE SPRINKLE CARD

With a pencil, lightly spell the word JOY on the front of a blank card. Use double-stick tape to make the letters, cutting the tape to fit and leaving the sticky side out. Pour small sprinkles on top of the tape. Shake off the excess.

FOR THE WASHI-TAPE CARD

Apply strips of washi tape to the front of the card and on the flap of the envelope, trimming excess tape. Overlap slightly to create unique designs. When complete, attach felt letters to the front using crafts glue.

VINTAGE ORNAMENT DISPLAY

Green vintage sherbet cups such as depression glass are the perfect size to display special ornaments. Group them together for a perfectly simple centerpiece.

PAINT CHIP TREES

Choose your favorite colors of green paint sample swatches and cut them into triangles.
Cut little trunks from shades of brown and arrange on a blank greeting card. Add a
simple message sticker and you have a perfect holiday card.

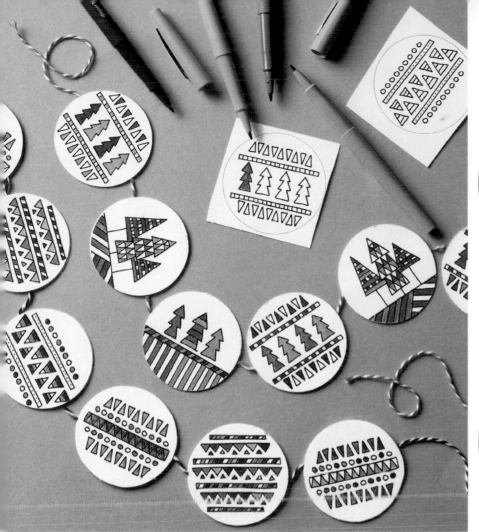

COLOR-ME GARLAND

Copy our little circles of holiday cheer, above, and use colored pencils or markers to color in the shapes. Lay the finished pieces in groups of two, with blank sides together, and lay a string or twine between each set. Glue together and let dry for a quick-and-colorful garland.

FUN STAMPS

Bring kids of all ages into the act with a collection of holiday stamps and bright ink pads, readily available online and at crafts stores. Use them to personalize gift wrap, handmade holiday cards, and fabric decorations.

SWEET SACHETS

Make a holiday display with just a few stitches and some red-and-white towels or red-striped vintage grain sacks. Cut square pieces, sew them right sides together, leaving a place to turn. Turn and stuff with fiberfill and whatever scent you like to create sweet sachets to tuck among holiday boughs.

SIMPLE PAINT BALL TRIMS

Use your creative genius to make these quick-to-paint ornaments to showcase on the tree or in pretty bowls.

FOR THE FLECKED ORNAMENTS
WHAT YOU NEED
Ornaments • Craft paint • Water • Paintbrush • Clear spray paint • Ribbon

WHAT YOU DO
Mix three parts paint with one part water (add more water if needed). Fill paintbrush with paint and flick onto ornaments. When dry, seal with clear spray paint.

FOR THE GLOSSY/FROSTED ORNAMENTS
WHAT YOU NEED
Glossy ornaments and frosted spray paint or • Frosted ornaments and clear gloss spray paint • Painters tape

WHAT YOU DO
Wrap painters tape around the center of the ornament and seal off area that you want to remain unpainted. Spray with frosted or clear gloss spray paint (depending on ornament). Let dry. Add a ribbon if desired.

FOR THE TONAL COLOR BLOCKED ORNAMENTS
WHAT YOU NEED
Ornaments • Crafts paint in colors similar to ornaments • Painters tape • Foam brush • Clear spray paint

WHAT YOU DO
Wrap painters tape around the center of the ornament. Using a foam brush, paint the exposed portion of the ornament. Let dry. Seal with clear spray paint.

ROCKIN' THE STOCKING

Crochet a bevy of tiny stockings for an array of uses. Make them the stars of the table as party favors or place cards. String them with ribbon for a garland or employ them as gift toppers. So easy to make, you will be making them by the dozens!

WHAT YOU NEED

Medium-weight 100% cotton yarn: red, white, green
● Size G/7 (4.5-millimeter) crochet hook ● Yarn needle

Note: Each stocking is crocheted in the round. Start each round with ch 1. Always join the last stitch to the first one with a slip stitch. You can place a removable marker at the beginning of each round and move marker up as a round is completed. Stitches are worked under both loops of stitches in the previous round.

WHAT YOU DO

CROCHET THE TOE
Make adjustable ring (or magic ring).
Rnd 1: Ch 1, 8 sc in adjustable ring. Tighten the ring. Join to the first st (8 sts).
Rnd 2: Ch 1, 2 sc in each st around, sl st to first st (16 sts).
Rnd 3: Ch 1, *sc in next 3 sts, 2 sc in next st, rep from * around, sl st to first st (20 sts).
Rnds 4–5: Ch 1, sc in each st around, sl st to first st (20 sts). If changing colors, fasten off, cut yarn, and join new color.

CROCHET THE FOOT
Rnds 1–7: Sc in each st around, sl st to first st.
Fasten off, cut yarn, and join new color.

CROCHET THE HEEL
The heel is crocheted back and forth, turning after each row. Join yarn in the middle of the side of the foot, so the previous round endings are at the bottom of the foot.
Row 1: Sc in next 12 sts, turn (12 sts).
Row 2: Ch 1, sc in 2nd st, sc in next 9 sts, turn (10 sts).
Row 3: Ch 1, sc in 2nd st, sc in next 8 sts, turn (9 sts).
Row 4: Ch 1, sc in 2nd st, sc in next 2 sts, sc2tog, sc in next 3 sts, turn (7 sts).
Row 5: Ch 1, sc in 2nd st, sc in next st, sc2tog, sc in next 2 sts (5 sts).
Fasten off, cut yarn, and join new color.

CROCHET THE LEG
Crochet in the round.
Rnd 1: Pick up and crochet 10 sc around heel, 10 sc around top of the foot, sl st to first st (20 sts).
Rnd 2: Ch 1, sc in next 8 sts, *sc2tog, sc in next 3 sts, rep from * once, sc2tog, sl st to first st (17 sts).
Rnds 3–9: Ch 1, sc in each st around, sl st to first st (17 sts).
Fasten off, cut yarn, and join new color.

CROCHET THE CUFF
Rnd 1: Sc in each st around, or every 3 sts make a spike st (sc in row below the working row), sl st to first st (17 sts).
Rnd 2: Sl st around to the back of the leg, ch 9, sl st in same st, sl st to the end of the rnd.
Fasten off. Cut yarn. Weave in ends.

BEG	begin(ning)	**REP**	repeat
CH	chain	**RND(S)**	round(s)
CONT	continue	**SC**	single crochet
DC	double crochet	**SL ST**	slip stitch
HDC	half double crochet	**SP**	space
INC	increase	**ST(S)**	stitch(es)
LP(S)	loop(s)	**YO**	yarn over

HAPPY SMILING SNOWMEN

Shiny round ball ornaments are transformed into little snowmen with purchased hat, eyes, and mouth. Just make a nose from kids' clay and you have it made!

WHAT YOU NEED

Orange clay • White ball ornaments • Tacky crafts glue • Snowman eye and mouth kit or beads (See Sources, page 160) • Purchased snowman hat • Embellishments for hat and scarf, if desired • White glitter, optional

WHAT YOU DO

1. Make a carrot shape using the orange clay. Set aside to dry.
2. Position the ornament on a table or towel to hold in place. Referring to diagram, below, glue the eyes and mouth to the front. Let dry.
3. Decorate the hat as desired. Glue to the top of the ornament.
4. Glue the nose to the front of the ornaments. Dust with glitter, if desired.

CHALKBOARD MESSAGE WRAPS

Write the perfect holiday message on each package when you wrap your gifts in white paper trimmed with black scrapbook paper. Add a red ribbon and write your message on the package with white chalk.

COOL CONTRAST

Classic black and white keeps the Christmas spirit modern. Cookie cutters define the trees but each one is original. The technique is so simple you will want to make multiples for gifts and toppers.

WHAT YOU NEED

Parchment paper • Oven-bake polymer clay in white, such as Craft Smart brand • Clay roller or rolling pin • Tree-shape cookie cutters (optional) • Crafts knife • Bamboo skewer • Baking sheet • Acrylic paint: white and black • Artists brushes • Ribbon or twine

WHAT YOU DO

1. Break off a piece of polymer clay and place on parchment paper. Using a clay roller or rolling pin, roll clay to about ¼ inch thick.
2. Use cookie cutters to cut out trees or use a crafts knife to freehand-cut tree shapes.
3. Push the end of a bamboo skewer through each treetop to make a hole for hanging loop. Place trees on baking sheet.
4. Referring to manufacturer's instructions, bake the clay; cool completely. Carefully shave off edges of each ornament using a crafts knife.
5. Paint the ornaments white; let dry. Apply more coats of white, as needed, letting ornaments dry between coats.
6. Referring to photo, above, paint details on each tree using black; let dry. Tie ribbon or twine through the hole in each ornament for a hanging loop.

Countdown to Christmas

Advent calendars are a time-honored tradition for marking the days to Christmas. Enjoy these projects that guide you to craft a special advent calendar for you and yours.

ALL IN A ROW

This farmhouse-style advent calendar can be used year after year. Purchase muslin bags at crafts stores or make your own. Then use large number stamps and red fabric paint to stamp each bag from 1 to 25. Run a thread or string through the top of the bags and hang on sticks. Fill the bags with goodies for every day.

SNOWMAN GOODIE CUPS

Plain white paper cups are transformed into 25 jolly snowman to greet each day before Christmas.

WHAT YOU NEED (FOR ONE CUP)

Paper cups • Pipe cleaners cut in half to 6 inches • Hot-glue gun and glue sticks • Permanent markers, such as Sharpie • Felt in assorted colors (orange for nose, various for scarf) • Scissors • Pom-poms • Number stickers • Items to fill cups

WHAT YOU DO

1. Set the cup on a flat surface. Using a hot-glue gun, attach the pipe cleaner on each side of the top of the cup. When dry, attach pom poms to each side.
2. Cut a tiny triangle from orange felt and attach to the front with hot glue. Referring to the photo, above, draw eyes and mouth with permanent marker.
3. To make the scarf, cut an 11×½-inch strip of felt. Cut a few slits at the end to create frays. Wrap around the cup, securing with hot glue.
4. Put a number sticker from 1 through 25 on each cup. Fill the cup with treats.

TINY TREASURES CHRISTMAS IDEAS

An old frame and a piece of fabric are pressed into service to create an Advent calendar, opposite. We cut a piece of foam-core board to fit the frame, wrapped it in fabric, and inserted it into the frame. Tags and treasures are hung with pearl-head straight pins on cut pieces of paper numbered from 1 to 25.

FARMHOUSE FLAIR

Counting the days until Christmas is as easy as hanging a wreath. A wood-bead wreath moves down the tree to mark progress toward the holiday. Start with a white background and stencil black numbers from 1 to 25. Add a tiny brass nail above each number. Then make a ring using wood beads to move from number to number.

PIN WORTHY

This framed Advent calendar was created by wrapping foam-core board with a yard of linen fabric and popping it into a gilded vintage frame. Print numbers on tags and raid crafts leftovers for bits and baubles—such as vintage broaches, tiny bottlebrush trees, or sparkling faux greenery—to pin to the foam-core board for each day.

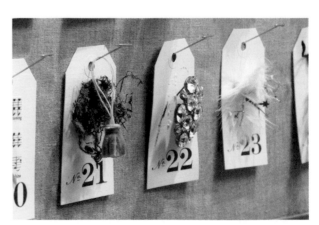

BOXED SET

Little paper boxes are dressed up for each day of Christmas. Start with purchased paper boxes with lids. Then paint the lids with your favorite colors of crafts paint. Using ribbons, twine, and tiny pom-poms, add embellishments to each box. Then fill them with little treasures to share. No matter the age, the anticipation of these little boxes will make the spirit bright.

NOTEWORTHY

*Deck the walls with this framed Advent calendar that
uses miniature numbered envelopes and note cards.
Each note features an inspirational message, a fun
holiday to-do, and for-the-love-of-family tidings tucked
inside envelopes in an assortment of papers. Add a mix
of handwritten and computer-printed numbers to the
envelopes and hang them from mini clothespins on ribbon
stretched across an empty picture frame.*

PINE CONES

This paper forest plays hide-and-peek with treats for a sweet Christmas countdown. Simply choose marbled decorative and scrapbook papers in a variety of greens (or your preferred palette). Roll the papers into 25 cones and secure each edge with double-stick tape. Using a circle punch or scissors, create a label for each tree with printed or hand-lettered numbers. Tape labels to cone trees with double-stick tape and place a treat under each. Give your paper forest the scent of real pine by accenting your arrangement with fresh greens.

TABLETOP ETIQUETTE

Use this guide (and the illustration, right) to ensure that your holiday table is perfectly set.

DINNER PLATE
Place this large plate directly on the table in the absence of a charger.

SALAD PLATE
Set the salad plate atop the dinner plate. It should be removed after the salad course is eaten.

SOUP BOWL
If soup is being served, place the bowl on the salad plate.

BREAD PLATE
Place this small plate, slightly larger than a saucer, above and to the left of the dinner plate (directly above the forks).

DINNER FORK
Set the large dinner fork to the immediate left of the dinner plate.

SALAD FORK
Because the salad fork is used first, place it on the outside—to the left of the dinner fork.

DINNER KNIFE
The dinner knife goes to the immediate right of the dinner plate, with the blade facing inward.

TEASPOON
Place the teaspoon to the right of the dinner knife, with the bowl facing up.

SOUP SPOON
If soup is being served, the soup spoon should sit to the right of the teaspoon.

DINNER NAPKIN
Place the dinner napkin to the left of the salad fork. For a more casual presentation (or if you're not using a soup bowl), place it on the salad plate.

WATER GLASS
Place this glass in easy reach above the dinner plate. Fill it with chilled water before guests are seated.

CHAMPAGNE FLUTE
Situate the champagne flute to the right of the water glass—between it and the and wine glass. The flute's tall and narrow shape keeps the champagne bubbly.

WINE GLASS
Place the wine glass to the right of the champagne flute. A red-wine glass is larger than a white-wine glass; its large bowl allows the wine to breathe.

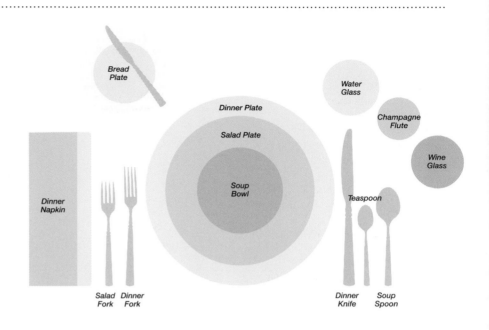

Bread Plate · Water Glass · Champagne Flute · Wine Glass · Dinner Plate · Salad Plate · Soup Bowl · Dinner Napkin · Teaspoon · Salad Fork · Dinner Fork · Dinner Knife · Soup Spoon

ENTERTAINING TIPS FROM THE PROS

SET IT AND FORGET IT
Set the table up to two days ahead and then cover it with a clean bedsheet to keep the dishes and glasses from gathering dust. This will give you more time on the day of the party to fine-tune the table decorations.

MAKE GLASSWARE SPARKLE
Avoid dusty or spotty surprises from drinking glasses pulled out at the last minute. Run glasses through the dishwasher before setting the table to make them sparkle. Hand-wash delicate items in advance too.

MEASURE UP
Let the tablecloth drop 12 to 18 inches from the edges of the table. (Use a silence cloth or pad beneath the cloth to protect the table.) Leave 12 inches between place settings. The dinner plate (or charger) and flatware should sit 1 inch from the edge of the table.

LET THE FOOD DO THE TALKING
Avoid using highly scented flowers or candles on the table. They interfere with the aromas and flavors of the food—plus some guests may be sensitive to certain flowers or perfumed candles.

KEEP SIGHT LINES OPEN
Centerpieces should be below eye level of seated guests—and flaming candles above—so diners can talk across the table easily. **Quick Tip:** Freeze candles before lighting them to prevent messy drips.

CHANGE IT UP
Consider serving dessert somewhere other than at the dining table, such as in the living room (in front of a crackling fire) or a four-season sunroom. Guests will be able to move around a bit before the final bites.

INDEX

STITCH DIAGRAMS

Backstitch

Straight Stitch

Chain Stitch

Whipstitch

French Knot

Buttonhole Stitch

Running Stitch

Stem Stitch

Star Stitch

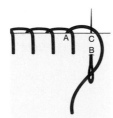

Blanket Stitch

KNITTING ABBREVIATIONS

BEG	begin (ning)
DEC	decrease
INC	increase
K	knit
LP	loop
M1	make one or to increase one
P	purl
SSK	slip, slip knit
TOG	together

SOURCES

Bakers Twine
hobbylobby.com

Birch Bark
Natural Birch Bark/amazon.com

Birds
lwingflyer/amazon.com

Candle Molds
candle molds/amazon.com

Cardstock/Scrapbooking Supplies
memoryboundscrapbookstore.com

Crafts Paint
deltacreative.com

Felt
National Nonwovens
nationalnonwovens.com

Flower Punch
EKSuccess
amazon.com

Gingerbread House Beads
Hilde & Joy/JoAnn's Fabrics

Glue
Aleene's Tacky Glue
aleenes.com

Papers and Stickers
memoryboundscrapbookstore.com
michaels.com

Paper Tape/Ribbon
hobbylobby.com
michaels.com

Paper-Wrapped Floral Stems
michaels.com

Ribbon
offray.com

Snowman face kit/hat
hobbylobby.com

Wire Wreath Form
Sumind 4 Wire/amazon.com

Wood Slices/Wood Pieces
michaels.com
woodcrafter.com

Wool Pom-Poms
craftywoolfelt.com

Yarn
yarnspirations.com

CROCHET ABBREVIATIONS

BEG	begin(ning)
CH	chain
DC	double crochet
HDC	half double crochet
INC	increase
SC	single crochet
SL ST	slip stitch
ST(S	stitch(es)

CRAFT DESIGNERS

Judy Bailey • Lindsay Berger • Jan Carlson •
Carol Field Dahlstrom • Roger H. Dahlstrom •
Chrissie Grace • Krystyna Herczak • Pam Koelling •
Katie Neighbour • Mathew Mead • Janet Pittman •
Reets, Reets to Stitches • Karla Taverna • Jan Temeyer